YOUNG Man

**A young man's guide
to teenage sexuality**

All Bible quotations are taken from the
Good News Bible unless otherwise
indicated.

Scriptures quoted from the *Good News
Bible* published by The Bible
Societies/HarperCollins Publishers Ltd.,
UK, © American Bible Society, 1966, 1971,
1976, 1992.

Scriptures quoted from the Holy Bible *New
International Version* published by Hodder
and Stoughton Ltd, UK, © New York
International Bible Society.

ISBN 1-873796-64-1

Printed in Bangkok for
Autumn House Publications
Grantham, England

Reprinted 1998, 2001 and 2003

YOUNG Man

Jonathan and Ana Gallagher
have considerable experience in
teenage, family and marriage
counselling. They live in
Hertfordshire, England, with their
two teenage children.

Jonathan Gallagher has degrees in
both the sciences and theology. He
has a PhD from the University of
St Andrews, Scotland. He is widely
known for his stimulating seminars
and lectures on Sexuality in Teenage
Years, and enjoys working with
young people.

Editor
DAVID MARSHALL
BA, PhD.

Medical Editor
EILEEN BAILDAM
MB, ChB, DCH, MRCGP, MRCP.

A young man's guide to teenage sexuality

WHY WE WROTE IT

Please make it real! That's what the young people said to us when they heard we'd been asked to write on teenage sexuality from a Christian viewpoint. Seems that they thought some books on the subject were silly or ridiculous. They wanted it spelled out; not only what was the Christian position, but why.

So this is it! We've included much information from the teens themselves, and teens are the ones who are asking the questions. The question and answer sessions at the end of the chapters come from the seminars on sexuality and intimate relationships that we've conducted over the years. They are genuine questions, the ones that real teens are asking.

For it's in the area of sexuality that the Christian view is most opposed to that of modern society. The pressures to follow 'the ways of the world' are great, and we must have true biblical answers that make sense to the youth of today.

That's why this book is specially for you. We have tried to make it personal, and to be practical, dealing with the real issues. We have dared to be very frank, because we believe that you want honest answers that do not talk around the subject, but confront it head-on. If this upsets some, we're sorry. But we are convinced that such an approach is the only way!

We hope that we have given some helpful answers to these questions, and some good reasons for the Christian view of sex. Most of all, we wish you the same kind of happiness we have experienced in all the many years we have been together, from the beginnings of love right up to the mature and deep love we still share.

JONATHAN AND ANA GALLAGHER

YOUNG Man

CONTENTS

1   PAGE 8

Sex is all around

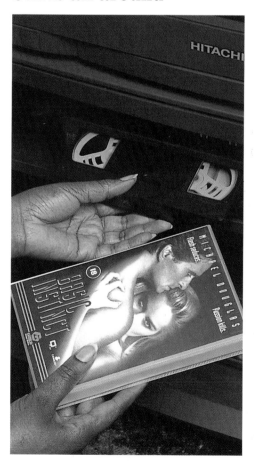

2   PAGE 19

Am I so strange?

3   PAGE 35

Mechanics!

4 PAGE 52

So what's it all about?

5 PAGE 67

Don't believe all you hear!

6 PAGE 78

Dealing with relationships

YOUNG
Man

7 PAGE 84

Sexuality – God's gift

8

Weary of the theory?

9 PAGE 117

When it all goes wrong

10 PAGE 132

Sexual distortions

11 PAGE 146

SEX the unhealthiest 'game'

12 PAGE 164

Ending guilt, becoming free

13 PAGE 177

The God of hope and healing

1

Sex is all around

Do not conform yourselves to the standards of this world, but let God transform you inwardly by a complete change of your mind. Romans 12:2.

EVERYWHERE

In the eyes. In the smiles. In the looks of girls in magazines and in the adverts. Saying, 'Come on. Sex is OK. Don't fight it — just enjoy it.' That's the message; and you'd have to be deaf and blind not to notice.

Sex is on the lips of others, some trying to persuade you to go their way. Sex is in the language, the jokes, the off-colour remarks. Sex is all around.

Ours is a world in which sex is used and abused and paraded. Made to seem the only way to have a happy life. Sex sells.

Inviting (human female) models draped across the latest (car) models. For what? To catch the eye? You *know* what it's all about. The 'swimwear' calendars. The lingerie adverts. The billboards. And even the girl who eats chocolate bars or licks her lips over yoghurt or who tries to make even washing powder look sexy!

Or the idea that when you go out with a girl, to have fun you must have sex. The belief that sex makes you a man. The stories that your friends tell you about their sexual activities (often made up!).

AN EXCESS OF SEX . . .

So much so that you'd think that just about any and all kind of sex is normal.

Or you're told that sex is wrong, but everybody does it. In the daylight people are the proper gentlemen and ladies, but after dark . . . .

NORMAL?

And why is the media so full of such obvious self-contradictions? They talk up fun sex and then hypocritically censure those caught in some kind of sexual indiscretion.

> **Today's world: 'The crime-ridden, sex-ridden, fear-ridden and sensually unstable society.'**
> *MALCOLM MUGGERIDGE*

Sex is all around. And not just in the papers and magazines, the ads and the movies, the TV and videos. In reality too.

In the current fashions. The briefest of swimsuits, micro-skirts, boob tubes, low-cut blouses and high cut dresses — just walk into the town . . . . Today's fashion seems dedicated to using the least to accentuate the most! Or is this just being a prude who wants to stop people having fun?

And we have only discussed what you can *see!*

What about the things you read and hear — the books and magazines and gossip and radio and . . . . Sexual stimuli seem to be ever-present in our modern culture, always ready to excite and indulge.

SEX IN POP SONGS

Just listen to the lyrics (and heavy breathing) and nothing is left to the imagination. Sex in its crudest form as a way of making sales. Sex as big business. Sex as commodity.

Reports about pornography being spread through the computer systems. The continuing increase in sex crimes. Marriages breaking down. Prostitution on the increase. Sex tourism. AIDS. Abortions.

The down side of sex is there for all to see. Why is all this? Because sex is ripped from its context of mutual love and sold or exploited or depraved.

Take away ideas of commitment and self-imposed restraint and then add an over-emphasis on the physical, and you end up with people preoccupied with selfish sensuality. In the words of Edward Carpenter:

From cars to photocopiers, bicycles to bread, sex is the popular marketing ingredient with the sensual invitation — buy me!

'Sex today is slimed over with the thought of pleasure.'

THE SENSUAL SOCIETY

For today's concepts of society are based on the sensual. 'Feeling good.' 'Do as you please.' 'Let yourself go.' 'It's your life!' 'I do what I like, it's a free country.' The individualistic, pleasure-seeking philosophy in which self is number one.

And so we are led into the search for physical excitement as the answer to our aching emptiness. As if sex can be a replacement 'religion' where we become eternally happy and find our true meaning and purpose in life! Commenting on this change in our 'religious' thinking, Malcolm Muggeridge expressed it well: 'The orgasm has replaced the Cross as the focus of longing and the image of fulfilment.'

How sad that a few moments of physical pleasure become the greatest objective, the one thing that is supposed to be truly meaningful! Yes, sex is wonderful, but it cannot be a life-philosophy. If we replace God with sex then we are not far from the pagan Canaanites and their fertility religions, and we animalize our natures. In a later chapter we'll look more at religion and sex, but for the moment recognize the way in which our society is changing, and the more and more obvious reliance on sexual pleasure as the great life goal.

Why is it that the highest compliment is to be sexy? How come so many guys spend hours fantasizing about sex? Why is sexual reality so different from sexual expectation? Where do all these sexual thoughts come from? How can such blatant sexual approaches be avoided?

So many questions! Now more than ever sex is at the top of the agenda, and Christians need to be dealing openly and honestly with the queries that are raised.

BEING MACHO

Macho ideas suggest that to be a man you have to pressurize a girl to have sex. That you need to exploit situations sexually. That to be a red-blooded male you must have a record of sexual conquests. The duty for any male presented with an opportunity for sex is that he is supposed to perform! Such preconceptions may lead you to do things you had not intended, but felt that they were expected of you.

One young man described going out with a girl who innocently told him she was on the pill. The guy took that to be a sexual invitation. Turned out later that she had been prescribed the pill to take care of her very heavy periods. You don't have to think much to see how that situation could have led to tragedy based on a misunderstanding.

See how you can tell yourself: 'She's willing, and is inviting me. So

So you're the sort of male who makes continual conquests because it's expected of you. Don't be fooled, you are a victim of propaganda that sells you short on relationships and satisfaction.

I don't have any choice. Even if I wanted to say "No", what would she think of me if I turned her down. And then what about my mates who might find out. They'd say I was impotent or worse. So I have to prove to her, to my friends, and to myself that I am a real heterosexual guy, a sexual athlete who can satisfy any girl who asks.'

Or you can say, 'I'm in love. I want to have sex. So if she is asking me, how can I refuse? Love needs to be demonstrated. She's made her decision, and if I don't say "Yes", then maybe she'll go elsewhere for her sexual satisfaction.'

See how the ideas of society control you! No one is totally immune from the conditioning of their background and experience. And because we live in such a sexual society, which is not just permissive but even attempts to force ideas of sexual promiscuity on us, then to be restrained and self-controlled is that much harder. It's in the area of sex that the Christian and the world are furthest apart — which can lead to many misunderstandings and much confusion.

DON'T BE FOOLED

So first major point: Don't be fooled by modern society's ideas about sex. We'll come back to that major theme in a later chapter. For now just make sure you're not blindly accepting other peoples' ideas. We need to go back to the beginning, and see the God who cre-ated our sexuality. The distorted sexual concepts that are so frequent today are not to be used as the baseline for Christians.

Ask yourself, 'Where do my ideas about sex come from?' If you're honest, most of them come from those around you — from your friends, the way you see sex portrayed in movies, the attitudes to sex you've absorbed unconsciously as you've grown up. But just because it may *seem* OK to think in a certain way, that doesn't necessarily make it right! Maybe we all have a lot to unlearn too.

We think particularly of a friend of ours who had experimented early with casual sex. He'd tell stories of what happened with all kinds of girls — and of course was generally admired for his sexual abilities. He'd gone from 'being in love' to 'having sex' — and jumped from one bed to the next like some sex-crazed butterfly. But despite all the bravado and the hype, he knew he was missing something. Sex certainly didn't solve his problems; quite the opposite. His work suffered; he was plagued by former girl-friends; he was often irritable and nervous. It was as if he realized that what he was doing wasn't helping, but that somehow he had trapped himself.

Admired as a Don Juan by many of his male friends, he was, deep down, a very insecure and troubled person. Maybe that had led him into sexual experimentation in the first place. But his sexual experiences cer-

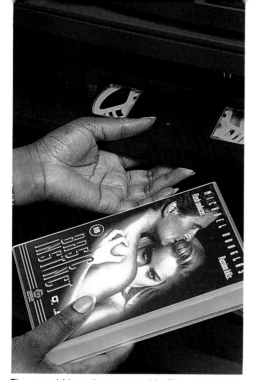

The sexual ideas demonstrated in films and videos provide a distorted and dishonest view which has become accepted as normal behaviour.

tainly hadn't helped. He never managed to form a good and lasting relationship with any woman and, to this day, remains a kind of 'sexaholic' — addicted to sex and yet damaged by it, continuing a habit of self-inflicted sexual abuse with no prospect of happiness.

What Raymond Chandler wrote about alcohol is also true of sex: 'Alcohol is like love: the first kiss is magic, the second is intimate, the third is routine. After that you just take the girl's clothes off.' Terrible proof of the casual and superficial attitudes to sex which treat women as objects with which to satisfy desire, as a collection of body parts, as some kind of mechanical device to please your sexual urges.

TRIVIAL SEX

Today, sexual intercourse as part of a boy-girl relationship is seen as ordinary and commonplace. Trivial sex — without commitment, without responsibility, without obligation — hardly raises any eyebrows either. The right to demand sexual satisfaction at a moment's notice seems to have been accepted by the majority without much argument. The result is 'The barren and heartless sexology which pollutes our moral and social environment today'. (Mary Whitehouse.)

Barren and heartless; such terms well summarize the wasteland of modern relationships in which genuine love and caring, of selfless generosity and concern for others has been thrown out of the window.

One of the effects of the 'sexual revolution' has been the use of women as objects for sexual exploitation.

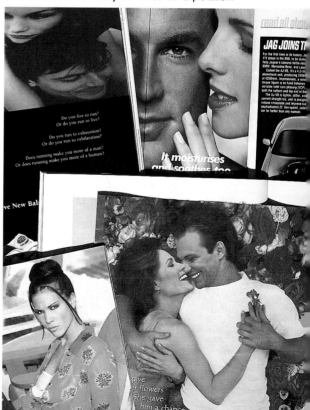

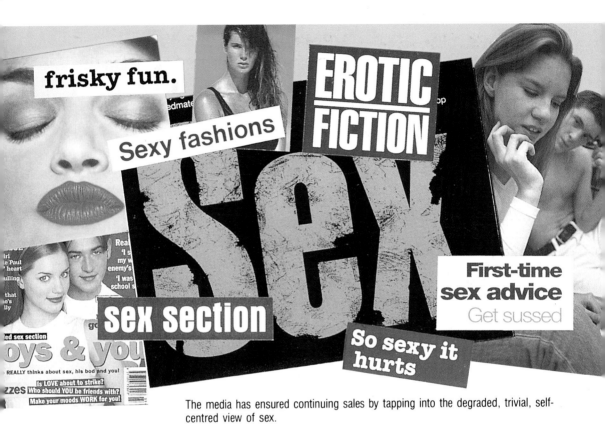

frisky fun.

Sexy fashions

EROTIC FICTION

First-time sex advice

Get sussed

sex section

So sexy it hurts

The media has ensured continuing sales by tapping into the degraded, trivial, self-centred view of sex.

As someone once said, 'Sex is not a nice way to say hello.' But in a world that has little else, selfish sexual pleasure has become the degraded way we are. The challenge is to say something *different* from all of that heartless and trivial self-centred sex, to show that God's intention for sex is far better, higher and greater than any of us can imagine.

For in saying 'No' to all the sexual errors, the Christian is not saying 'No' to God's wonderful gift of sexuality. Christian sex is better sex, is more fulfilled sex, is far superior than that promoted by the sex-sick society.

It is our firm conviction that if Christians do not speak the truth about God-given sexuality then the Arch-liar will have his way. That the Church may have had wrong ideas, or has been silent too long, or may feel embarrassed, means that sexual evil has been spreading quickly, and almost without opposition.

You need to relate to your own sexuality, to channel and direct it wisely, and to learn fast too! You don't need to repeat everybody else's failings just to find out where to go wrong. Most importantly, don't let others tell you how to behave, and take God with you as you go.

QUESTIONS AND ANSWERS

Why do you think sex is so popular today?

Because it really can be a different kind of life-style. Instead of a religion of God, you can turn to a religion of selfish pleasure-seeking. And because so many people have given up on God, they look for other things to fill up their empty lives. Sexual thrills may be one way of doing this, although no deep satisfaction can be gained. Add to that the need to feel good about yourself, to brag to others, to think yourself a real man; it's easy to see how much time and energy can be wasted in chasing sexual pleasures. Of course, such ideas are not new. But in a world that is fast losing its way, sex becomes more and more popular, and is used and abused in just about every way you could ever imagine.

I can't see what's wrong with looking at beautiful women. That's today's society.

A common view. But let's look at it more closely. What are you thinking as you look? Admiring beauty is one thing; filling your mind with lust is another. Do you see the woman as a person you'd like to get to know, or just a collection of shapely legs, breasts, buttocks and so on? Where does the idea of respect come in? What kind of values are you operating from? Is the woman just a clothes-horse for a fashion display? Or is she someone you'd like to talk to and discuss and really relate to? See the difference? — it's very important.

Sex is just normal. Why stop yourself?

Two answers. One: eating is 'normal' but you control your appetite, unless you want to become grossly overweight. Just because something is called 'normal' doesn't mean it is appropriate. Two: do you want to be someone who is a slave to his desires? Are you so weak that you 'have' to do what your body says? Sex is wonderful, beautiful, marvellous — but only when it is right! Sex can also be destructive, terrible and boring. Sex is what you make it, not what it makes you.

Why should I be any different? Everybody else does it.

Do they? How do you know? A lot of boys brag about sex but have had no real experience. And then, do you just want to be part of the herd? Being different can be great — especially when you know you are right! Just because 'everybody else does it' is no reason for you to. In fact, quite the opposite, for in matters of sex the majority is usually wrong. Just think for a few moments, and try to see sex the way God does. You'll be less willing to trade in such a wonderful gift for the substitute sex that the world sells.

How can you fight it? I mean, everywhere I look I see SEX!

Maybe you need to watch where you're looking! OK, so sex is all around. But you don't have to go out and find it. You can choose what you fill your mind with. Thinking on the right things is the best start (see Philippians 4:8). Then you need to learn the facts about sex; how images excite, how ideas work. By understanding the way you react, you can begin to control your reactions. You don't need to give up before you start! God gave you the gift of sexuality, but He also gave you a mind to use, free choice, and ways to control your physical drives.

THE SEX TEST

This is a simple true or false test to help you see what your attitudes to sex really are. Answer the questions honestly, and if you can, get a few friends to take the test too. That way you can begin to examine your own thoughts and the attitudes of those around you too. But remember — it's not our own attitudes that decide what's true and right. Sex involves basic morality, and just because we think something is right or wrong doesn't make it so!

BASIC ATTITUDES

T F
☐ ☐ Sex is just for fun
☐ ☐ Sex is dirty
☐ ☐ Sex is just for making babies
☐ ☐ Sex is scary
☐ ☐ Sex is sin

CHRISTIANS AND SEX

T F
☐ ☐ Sex is a gift from God
☐ ☐ Christians and non-Christians should see sex the same way
☐ ☐ God isn't worried about the Christian's sex life
☐ ☐ God made us sexual so it's His fault
☐ ☐ I can't help sexual temptations

OUTSIDE INFLUENCES

T F
☐ ☐ Most people lie about their sex lives

☐ ☐ Sex is OK as long as no
one gets hurt

☐ ☐ Everybody else is having
sex, so what I do doesn't
matter

☐ ☐ I've learned what is right
and wrong about sex from
friends

☐ ☐ What I read and watch
affects my sexual values

SEXUAL SITUATIONS

T   F

☐ ☐ Heavy petting before
marriage is wrong

☐ ☐ Feeling guilty after sex
proves it was wrong

☐ ☐ Having sex is OK if you're
engaged

☐ ☐ Sexual sins are very
damaging

☐ ☐ To stay a virgin today is not
realistic

Now if you're like most people
who've taken this test, you want to
argue about some of the answers.
Because it's true that the answer you
give does depend on the exact
situation. For example, 'Sex is sin',
depends on whether you're married
or not, exactly what you mean by sex
(sexual intercourse, or just touching
each other), and exactly what you
mean by sin (is it against what God
has said, or just what you might
think is wrong. For example some
people believe any kind of
masturbation is wrong, but this is
not mentioned in the Bible). 'I can't
help sexual temptations' depends on
whether you think temptations are
wrong themselves, or whether you
believe you can't help yourself, and

what you should do about putting
yourself into a position to get
tempted! And some of the other
questions may have an 'It depends'
kind of answer.

But you should now have a better
idea of some of the issues you need
to sort out in your mind. That's
what we're going to do together in
this book.

Whether it is TV, films, magazines or any other
source of sex material, *you* have the means to
control its influence.

It's wise to find out whether your opinions on relationships and sex are based on truth or fiction!

WHAT I THINK

Here's what I think about sex and moral issues (Tick those you agree with, cross against those you disagree with)

☐ What I do sexually is nobody's business but my own.

☐ Using birth control is a Christian duty.

☐ The Church's ideas about sex are out of date.

☐ There are good reasons to wait until you're married before having sex.

☐ Abortion is wrong.

☐ The Bible doesn't mention oral sex so it must be OK.

☐ I agree with my parents' views about sex.

☐ God invented sex so it must be good.

☐ Other peoples' ideas about sex affect me.

☐ Sexual fantasies are OK as long as you don't do anything.

☐ Masturbation is a sin.

☐ My ideas about sex need improving.

☐ Girls who tease boys deserve all they get.

☐ Homosexuality is condemned by God.

☐ If you get a girl pregnant you should marry her.

☐ You can do anything you like sexually as long as you don't go all the way.

☐ Having two girl-friends at once is wrong.

☐ I believe in love at first sight.

☐ I really don't understand what sex is all about.

☐ I feel guilty about my sexual experiences.

2

Am I so strange?

So God created human beings, making them to be like himself. He created them male and female. Genesis 1:27.

NORMALITY

'I seem to think about sex a lot. Is this normal?' Perhaps from the guys that's the commonest kind of question we receive in conducting Sexual Relationship seminars. That and concern over appearance and attractiveness are the most frequent (who says girls are the only ones who are vain?). So the most important first statement is:

YOU ARE NORMAL!

Now that doesn't immediately mean that whatever you're doing is right. And you can't take it that you can blame your sexuality either. 'I couldn't help it — I'm just made that way' is no excuse.

But for teens sexual awareness and development is a very significant process, and especially in modern society it's not surprising that you may think about sex a great deal.

In dealing with guys and their problems it's always amazing how many think that they and they alone

have a particular problem. We don't say that wrong is right, or that because a majority does something it's acceptable (the 'It's OK — everybody does that' idea). But it is helpful to realize that certain problems and situations are part of growing up and that most people go through similar experiences.

We don't know whether it's because of culture or a real gender factor, but more boys than girls come to us with the idea that they're odd or strange. Perhaps the male ego is more fragile, perhaps they feel they have more to prove. Whatever — the feeling of being odd or unusual is quite common.

ON BEING MALE

Which is a good place to begin thinking about those intimate aspects of life that can sometimes seem so threatening. In the next chapter we'll look at the physical matters to do with sex. But for now

Where once girls were only a nuisance and stupid and shouldn't have been invented, now they seem to have a totally different appeal.

let's concentrate on you as a boy.

As you develop from childhood to manhood there are many changes you have to deal with. The basic question is one of identity: Who am I? As a child you were content with a child's life. But now you understand that there's much more to life than you saw as a child. Girls now have an interest for you — unlike before! And there's the whole mystery of love and sex and marriage. Add to that the need to make decisions about what kind of job to do and where to live — and the very questions of life itself, such as What is it all for? What is life's meaning, purpose and end? No wonder you may feel overwhelmed by the questions and choices facing you and how to respond.

And sometimes you may make

decisions which are not wise. You may not feel accepted by those you once called friends. Your appearance may change and you may be taunted about this. You may worry about how to relate to others, especially girls, and wonder how to fit into adult society.

You may also have concerns about your sexuality and normalness. Sadly in these days of sexual openness, doubts about sexual orientation can be exploited by those with a particular agenda. Just because you may have 'a crush' on another boy does not make you a homosexual, for example. In fact it is quite common in the adolescent years to form very close friendships with members of the same sex. So don't let others tell you you're strange!

Remember what the Bible says about being 'fearfully and wonderfully made'. You are very special. You are a unique individual, and you are loved and appreciated in your specialness by God Himself.

But back to the whole question of strangeness and normality. Often the idea 'I'm really strange' comes from not knowing that others have the same experiences. It's just that we don't talk about them.

DREAMING

For example, everyone has fantasies. They have day-dreams about what they would like to have happen. They dream about what they would like to own. They fantasize about all kinds of things, but most especially about love and sex. It is not wrong to have such thoughts. You are not sinning by wanting to experience this wonderful gift of God. The problems come only when fantasies go beyond what is good and pure and true and follow the perverted lies of the Devil.

Don't let anyone accuse you of deviant behaviour if your close friend is the same sex.

Since so many have problems here, let's illustrate. To dream about making love to a woman, to touch and caress and thrill with physical sexual expression is not wrong. You need to remind yourself that this is to be part of a committed relation-

Girls often appear more grown-up than boys. This can make you feel awkward or embarrassed, but after a while your sensitivity will actually help you relate.

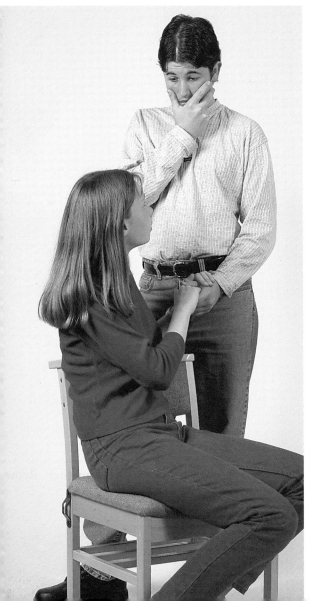

ship of marriage but, as the Song of Solomon shows, such thoughts and dreams can be very good.

On the other hand, if you were to fantasize, for example, about just seeking your own pleasure, about forcing a woman against her will, about sexual practices which God has expressly forbidden — then obviously this cannot be good and helpful.

While we cannot necessarily control what we dream about at night when we are asleep, we need to make sure that our fantasies and our day-dreams are ones which uplift sex and love, and not mirrors of the Devil's perverted ideas.

So feed your mind with good food, just as you do your body. Don't feed it with spicy stimulants or give it harmful drugs or make it drunk. Pornography does the same kind of thing to the mind. Dwelling on sexual perversions can do equivalent damage. So accept the gifts God gives for our pleasure, and don't abuse them.

FEARS

Some feeling of strangeness can also be due to social clumsiness — you get embarrassed or shy around girls. This can lead to fears about whether you may be homosexual (since you may feel happier around boys), or worries about whether you will be able to find a life partner.

Once again, most people have felt shy or embarrassed at some time. Even the most social of us have our

If you feel shy with girls forget the macho image stuff; just try talking about things that matter to you. With the right girl you will be surprised how easy it is.

Using aggressive behaviour as a means of impressing the girls is a pretty futile way of gaining their respect.

hidden fears. And as you grow up you are learning all the time. Don't expect to be able to fit into adult society straight away. Also bear in mind that in the teen years, girls do seem to be more mature in their ideas and judgements. The fact that you are sensitive to this is not a problem; your sensitivity helps you deal with your developing sexuality. Instead of trying to play the fool or put on a show, learn to become grown up and talk about things that really matter. Girls who are impressed by fast cars are not necessarily the best wives!

Anthony was a young teenager who was very concerned about himself, although he found it hard to express his feelings. He thought he was the only person in the world to be plagued with guilt and doubt. He needed to be helped to understand, accept and appreciate his sexuality. For much anxiety — even terror — can be removed through an understanding of who you really are.

As Anthony came to understand his needs and his drives, he worked his way through his feelings of insecurity. To be over-concerned about yourself can lead to real personality problems — like avoiding social contact, fear of girls, poor self-worth and so on.

The other extreme can be an over-reaction, where you have to try and prove yourself. Fights, dare-devil actions, competitions — all these are ways that boys try to prove (most of all to themselves) that they are 'all

YOU AND YOUR SEXUALITY

Tick the terms below that you think apply to you and your sexuality. (These are 'feeling' words and so may or may not be true. What is looked for here is your attitude to your own sexuality.)

healthy	worried	happy	strict	honest
scared	ashamed	dirty	appropriate	perverted
out-of-control	pure	good	harmful	unhealthy
proper	flirty	sad	biblical	embarrassed
guilty	virtuous	honourable	true	wrong
worthless	right	changeable	cheap	careful

right'. Of course this can be very dangerous, and may not help in overcoming feelings of weakness. The idea that 'I am imperfect, I am defective' in some way needs to be dealt with or the whole life may be damaged.

To become some macho he-man is not helpful. Nor is to become a kind of hermit who rarely goes out and who does not know how to relate to girls. Fears about penis size, how to please girls, worries about having no friends or wrong friends, loneliness, attractiveness — all these can ruin teenage development.

The important fact to recognize is that everyone has concerns over their identity and abilities. You just need to be yourself; not to be too worried about how you look; and try to develop friendships with both boys and girls together. Remember, there's no rush, and don't be pressurized by what others are doing.

Most of all recognize that you are a special person in God's eyes. He has made you, and knows you better than you do yourself. You can share your worries with Him; and He is

Shutting yourself away will not help you understand or relate to girls.

HOW YOU SEE YOURSELF

Underline all the words that you think describe how you look (on the outside — physical appearance is what we're talking about here).

handsome	charming	odd	fat	athletic
ugly	short	tall	oversexed	attractive
tough	silly	repulsive	thin	funny
perfect	ordinary	seductive	wiry	small
graceful	sexy	elegant	useless	masculine
pleasant	nasty	rugged	lovable	sleek
good	disgusting	firm	pitiful	dull

always totally reliable. If you do have some definite anxieties then you can always talk to a mature counsellor whom you trust. And live life looking for the good.

TAKE TIME TO THINK

We live in an unthinking age. 'Just do it. If it feels good, don't ask questions. And do it now!' That's the advice today.

But such advice is terribly destructive. Sex is not something for the immature. And the sad facts are that all too many young men have experimented with sex far too soon, and have been burned.

A recent survey on sexual behaviour in Britain (*Sunday Review*, 16 January 1994) reveals that, of the latest generation to become sexually active (those boys born in the early 1970s), half had lost their virginity at 17 and a quarter by the age of 15. This is no kind of encouragement; rather these are depressing statistics that reveal just how far the sexual revolution has come. That so many under-age boys should be experiencing sexual intercourse is a matter of great concern. Is it really likely that they will be able to form good and stable relationships at that age, and do they know what they are doing?

Sex doesn't 'make you a man'. That foolish statement has caused much grief. What makes you a man is the ability to make your own decisions for yourself, to choose your own life. And sex is only safe in a marriage relationship, when you are really mature enough to handle it.

To have sexual thoughts, to find yourself becoming sexually aware, and to be developing sexually is normal. The real test is what you do with this new experience. Are you a real man? Can you handle sex wisely?

Some feel pushed out of the running by hunky good-looking fellows who don't have problems in attracting girls. In the end it is personality, kindness and commitment that make long-term relationships.

QUESTIONS AND ANSWERS

I feel sexually excited by seeing my girl-friend in a swim-suit. Is that wrong?

Not in itself. All that proves is that your mental and physical 'wiring' is working properly. How you react to this experience is more important. If you allow your sexual thoughts to take over and lead you, then you'll have problems. Fire is of great use when it is handled carefully and properly controlled. When fire is out of control, it can become a monster that destroys everything in its path. So be aware of what is happening, and make sure that you are in control, and not your burning desires. And be careful that this doesn't turn into lust — which is greedy sexual passion for some *thing*. Love sees the other as a person; lust just sees an object. And no woman wants to be turned into an object!

These days should a man feel that he should be the dominant partner within a relationship or marriage? Or should there be equal status within the relationship?

As Jesus said to those who asked Him about marriage relationships in His day, 'In the beginning it was not so.' Eve is clearly described as a 'help-meet' for Adam. Not a slave, or someone to lord it over, but as an equal but different partner in marriage. Different cultures have gone away from this ideal. But if you are to have a happy marriage you both need to come to an agreement as to how your relationship will work — and not follow what you're told *should* happen. That doesn't mean you have to accept the way the world works either — you need to decide for yourselves.

I think I look ugly and to prove it no girl ever wants to go out with me. I can't see myself ever having a girl-friend.

Attractiveness is not just physical — remember that. And beauty is in the eye of the beholder! Besides, would you really want a girl-friend who only wants you for your outward appearance? Of course, the way things work is through physical attraction at first. But don't put yourself down. Be yourself, for eventually the inner beauty of a good character is worth far more than physical attractiveness. Go out in a crowd, and develop friendships. Your time will come!

I catch myself looking at girls and then feel guilty about it. Is it really wrong to want to look?

Again the answer is, 'It depends.' It depends on what you're thinking, and whether this is in harmony with what is good or not. Remember Jesus gave the legalists of His time a hard statement that anyone who looked with lust on a woman had committed adultery with her in his heart (see Matthew 5:27, 28). That was not to scare, but to make these men aware that just because they weren't actually *doing* anything did not make their hearts pure. It seems they believed you could think all kinds of disgusting sexual thoughts, but that was all right because nothing happened. Jesus shows us that we can sin in our minds too, and just because no one else sees doesn't make it OK, for such inner sins can do us just as much damage. But if your looking is just curiosity and natural attraction, then there's nothing wrong. The opposite is bad too — don't feel guilty about something that is not sinful.

Why do I always feel so threatened when a girl talks to me?

Maybe you aren't used to female company. Maybe you have certain ideas of how a boy relates to a girl. Maybe you have been frightened off by the talk of some of your friends. The important thing is that just because a girl talks to you, this doesn't mean that she wants to go out with you, or begin a serious relationship. Talk is just talk, and you can keep it on a surface level if you want. Just answer the questions, and treat the girl like a normal human being. Obviously you talk to others normally, like your family and friends. Discuss school work, or holidays, or even the weather. Don't see every girl as a potential partner. Don't have too many expectations. Just don't take it so seriously —

To be attracted to a good looking girl is quite natural, it doesn't have to be wrong — it depends on you and your motives.

lighten up! And if you're shy, go along as part of a group.

A girl I like caught me looking down her blouse. Now every time I see her I go red and feel embarrassed. How can I explain that I really do like her?

Whoops! You need to backtrack and make sure she realizes you are interested in more than her body. Now it may well be that she appreciated the fact that you found her physically attractive (most human beings are flattered by such attention!). And you may need to consider what you think — because the fact that you are now embarrassed suggests that you realize that what you were thinking was not entirely appropriate. There's nothing wrong in being physically attracted to girls, but remember that any relationship must be based on more than this. If you really are interested in her as a person, try to get to know her, discover mutual interests, and look her in the eyes rather than anywhere else.

My friends say I'll only be a man if I do it to a girl. But that's not what it says in the Bible. I don't want to seem a wimp, but I don't want to do anything evil either. Could you comment please.

Don't be foolish. Your friends are hardly good friends to suggest this. You don't need to prove your manhood to anybody. As you say, that's not what God says, and is only a way to get you to sin. You're not a wimp if you resist such ideas. In fact a wimp is someone who can't handle pressure. And so it's

WHO AM I?

Tick the Yes or No boxes of the qualities that apply to you. Not about outward appearance, but the kind of person you believe you are.

CHECKING YOUR SELF-ESTEEM

YES NO

☐ ☐ I'm happy with myself.

☐ ☐ I accept much criticism against me.

☐ ☐ I worry a lot what people think of me.

☐ ☐ I know I'll never amount to much.

☐ ☐ People talk about me behind my back.

☐ ☐ I may not be perfect, but I'm OK.

☐ ☐ I'm preoccupied with what I look like.

☐ ☐ I kind of expect to fail my exams.

☐ ☐ I appreciate getting compliments.

☐ ☐ I know God loves me, even the way I am.

Now think about the answers you've given. They should give you some idea of the way you see yourself, and help you see where you need to change. Remember — you need to see yourself not as you are, but as you can be, with God's help.

guys who do as their friends say, or who can't handle their own sexual pressure, who are the real wimps. Since you need to be strong to resist such suggestions and your sexual drive, then be strong!

I have lots of spots on my face and I get teased a lot. I get pretty miserable and don't have a girl-friend. Do you have any advice on how to get one?

Physical attractiveness is not the most important thing. Most girls tell us that they are more interested in a guy who is friendly, considerate, helpful, kind and caring than someone who is a brainless hunk. The teasing probably comes more from the guys than the girls, who may be more sympathetic than you think. The tendency is to feel self-conscious and stay away from people. This is the worst thing to do. Go to your doctor or the chemist for some medication for your spots, and don't be put off. Show your inner self, and make good friends who won't put you down.

I get lonely and then I find myself tempted with bad thoughts. How can I get rid of them?

Not by concentrating on them, that's for sure! That's the problem. The more you think about bad thoughts, the more they dominate your life. You say that you're lonely, and that is a factor. Having too much time to fantasize is a problem, and so you need to develop other interests. Spend more time with others, think of how you can get involved — maybe in church youth activities, or community work, etc.

As well as a route to physical fitness, sport is an excellent way of making new friends and a means of concentrating the mind.

The only way to 'get rid of bad thoughts' as you put it is to crowd them out with good ones. Overcome evil with good, don't concentrate on the evil.

OPINIONS

ROBERT
Lots of my friends boast about what they've done with girls. But most of the time I don't believe them. I don't know why it's supposed to be so great to sleep around. I think it's really stupid, and dangerous too.

AGREE/DISAGREE

COMMENT

JOHN
I find myself thinking about sex a lot. I try not to, but it's really hard, especially the way some girls dress. I mean, it's as if they are really trying to tempt me.

AGREE/DISAGREE

COMMENT

DAVID
If I'm honest, I get nervous about girls. I worry that they may expect me to have sex, and I don't know if I want to do that. I'm still a virgin, and even though I'm curious about sex, I would really like to wait until I get married.

AGREE/DISAGREE

COMMENT

DON
I've been out with plenty of girls. And if they don't want to do it, then I'm not interested. Sex has got to be part of any relationship I have.

AGREE/DISAGREE

COMMENT

THOMAS
I really don't understand about girls. They give you a come-on look, and then when you get all excited they don't want to know. I think they should stop teasing boys. We're only human, and it's hard to stop once you've started.

AGREE/DISAGREE

COMMENT

STEVE
I have many girls as friends, but I find it easy to make it clear that I don't believe in sex before marriage. My current girl-friend is great, and she wants to wait too. It can get difficult sometimes, but you just have to be strong and not get into tough situations.

AGREE/DISAGREE

COMMENT

TONY

If you're in love, sex comes naturally. So I don't think you should fight it. If it feels right, then why say it's wrong?

AGREE/DISAGREE

COMMENT

WHAT GIRLS WISH

I wish boys would treat me as me. I wish I could find someone who really cared about me, and not about the way I look. Especially because I have rather large breasts, the only thing boys want to do is to look and touch them. Sometimes I feel like asking whether they are kids who want to play with balloons. I mean, I'm more than that, and I wish the boys could see that.

I wish boys would try to talk more. Often they just don't say anything, and that can be really embarrassing. They think that all you should do is kiss and all that, but I want to have proper conversations.

Most guys who ask me out are interested in just one thing, even those who call themselves Christian. I get really fed up being pushed to have sex all the time, and I wish that they could understand that. I want to have a good relationship, and to do things together. But they only want to do one thing.

I wish boys were a bit more caring. Most of them say they're in love, but don't really mean it. I've been let down so many times I'm getting really fed up with it. So I'm very careful who I go out with, and make it clear where I stand. I'm more interested in friendship right now.

I wish boys wouldn't get me going. I get turned on very easily, and find it so hard not to get carried away. Because boys rely on girls to say 'No', I find it really difficult. They should take their share of the responsibility. Girls are human too!

3

Mechanics!

**I praise you because I am fearfully and wonderfully made.
Psalm 139:14, NIV.**

PHYSICS

From everywhere you're being bombarded with ideas and definitions about sex. Even the word 'sex' has different connotations and meanings depending on who you're talking to. For many people it can be a most confusing subject. So we need to talk very directly about the specific and physical aspects of sex — to get rid of all the falsehoods and old wives' tales. And none of the talking round the subject or assuming the obvious, or using vague old expressions like 'passing on the torch of life'! Only by being frank and open will we progress in our sexual attitudes and behaviour.

If some aspects of the physics of sex upsets, just remember who created and made our bodies. The fact that we may have perverted and corrupted the ideal does not mean that our bodies are wrong or evil. Let's not joke around either, or cover embarrassment by speaking in a cheap way. We'll use the correct terms for the sexual organs, and not some slang or offensive words that seek to make sex dirty.

So where to begin?

For most males it's with the penis. In the mind that is the most sexual part, even though without the brain and thoughts sex would be as much fun as it seems for fish and worms.

The first preoccupation is one of size. Sideways looks in school changing rooms and elsewhere are the way of comparison, and the concerns begin:

'Am I normal? Is it big enough? Will I get laughed at for a small penis? Will it work properly — and how do I find out?'

So what is normal, in terms of size? When erect the average is about six to seven inches (about 15cm). Some may be larger, some smaller. But despite the preoccupation that men have with size, this is not significant to most women, or to the ability to have a good and healthy sexual life. And since there is little you can do to alter the size of your penis, it's certainly best to stop worrying about size right now. Only medical conditions in which the penis is severely underdeveloped should be real cause for concern.

And since the major female stimulation is associated with the clitoris that is situated outside the vagina, then length really is not an issue in bringing pleasure to the woman.

Another obvious difference is circumcision in which the foreskin (the outer skin covering the head of the penis) is removed. While the debate continues over whether this is more hygienic, there would seem to be no difference when it comes to sexual sensation. As long as the penis is properly washed then problems due to infection under the foreskin will be unlikely. Whether you are circumcised or not makes no difference to you or your partner's sexual fulfilment.

THE SEXUAL PARTS

So what is the penis and how does it work? Look at the illustration below (cross section of male genitals) and you'll see that the penis is mainly made up of spongy tissue that fills with blood when you have an erection ('get hard'). In its limp state the penis would not be able to penetrate the vagina, but once it is erect this becomes easy.

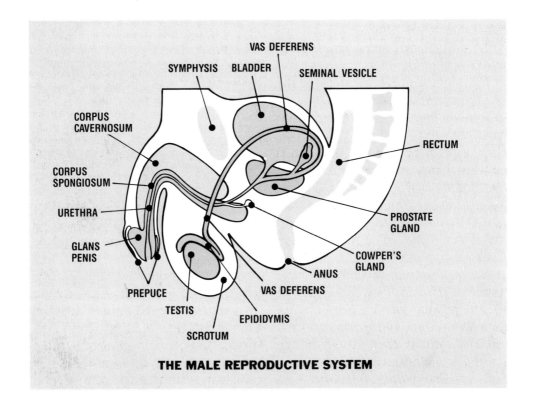

THE MALE REPRODUCTIVE SYSTEM

You may have noticed that having an erection is not necessarily associated with obvious sexual thoughts. Sometimes you may have an erection on waking in the morning. While uncomfortable occasionally, it is *not* true that sex then is essential. Only if you find yourself erect frequently and for long periods may there be a problem, and if this occurs ('priapism') you should consult your doctor.

Underneath the penis is the scrotum, the 'bag' that contains the two testicles. These have been designed to keep semen a little cooler than the normal body temperature, which is why the testicles are on the outside of the body. In the illustration you can see how the testicles are connected to the penis, and this is the path semen takes when ejaculation occurs.

The genitals are shown in the normal (flaccid) state.

You will have noticed changes that have occurred since childhood. This change from boy to youth is called puberty. Hormones begin to prepare the body sexually. The penis and testes enlarge, hair grows in the pubic area, under the arms, and on the face. The voice breaks and muscles develop. The male sex hormone testosterone produced by the testes is part of this process, and sperm production is begun. The testicles produce the sperms and the seminal fluid is then stored in the seminal vesicles until discharged.

Once these storage chambers are full semen is released, often at night in so called 'wet dreams' which may or may not be associated with erotic dreaming. These nocturnal emissions are quite natural and normal, and nothing to be worried about. Sometimes boys worry that they are doing something wrong, and that this is some kind of sin. On the contrary this is just the body's way of dealing with sperm production.

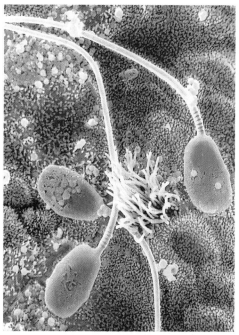
A highly magnified view of male sperm in the female uterus after ejaculation has taken place.

The sensation of this discharge (ejaculation) is pleasurable, and the dreams may be of sexual activity. This may also lead to conscious stimulation of the penis while awake to produce the same result. This is called masturbation, and we will talk about this in a later chapter.

Each ejaculation contains between two and four millilitres of this liquid called semen. This represents on average about 200 million sperms! Each of these sperms is theoretically able to fertilize a female egg and so produce a baby. Sometimes young teenagers are not even aware of this, and so it is important to emphasize that once you are able to produce

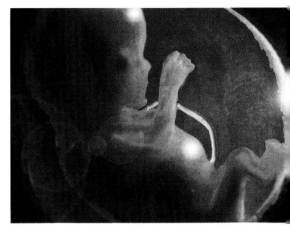

After five months the foetus has now developed into a fully formed infant.

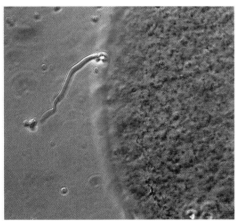

A male sperm fertilizes an egg from the female ovary.

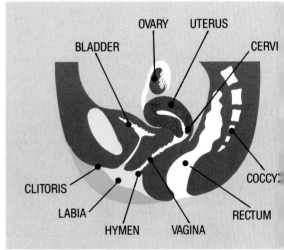

A cross section through the vagina and the uterus — as if you were looking from one side.

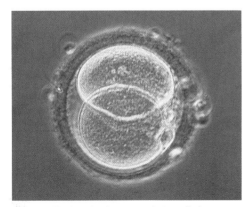

After fertilization the human embryo called a zygote starts dividing into multiple cells.

sperm you can make a girl pregnant.

The illustration above shows the female genitals. You need to be aware of the female sexual organs, not as an incentive to improper experimentation, but to be aware of how sex works for her too. By understanding what is going on, you will at least be able to recognize the stages of sexual stimulation and be able to stop before things get out of hand.

Fertilization occurs when a sperm meets an ovum, normally in the uterus. The ovum is produced once a month during the regular cycle by one of two ovaries. Each ovary contains 250,000 to 500,000 ova. Just why we need so many potential eggs or so many millions of sperm is a mystery — but it shows the wonderful provision the Creator has made for sexual reproduction.

Once fertilization has occurred this cell begins to grow and develop through one of the most marvellous miracles of life, until nine months later a baby is born.

SEX: THE STEP PROCESS

An essential fact about sexual activity is that one thing really does lead to another. You need to know this! Otherwise you can so easily be caught out, because one action moves smoothly to another. But realizing this can help you to stop before it is too late.

It's like a ladder. Each step may seem small, but before you know it you're swaying dizzily at the top, wondering how you got there. So let's look at the steps.

Step one. Some kind of mutual attraction. Maybe it was eyes meeting across a crowded room, as the saying goes. A smile, and you smiled back. Something like that. A recognition of liking.

Step two. Contact! Somewhere, somehow, somewhen. Your arms 'accidentally' touch. Or you shake hands even. Some touch which may seem entirely normal, but which you both recognize as being different.

Step three. Touch that is a real demonstration of affection. You hold hands. You hug each other maybe. All of which is a prelude to

Step four. A kiss. Just a kiss. But a very definite step up the ladder of sexual involvement. Because this is not a kiss like greeting Mum. And you both know it.

Step five. The kissing gets longer and deeper. 'French kissing' (tongue into the partner's mouth) may occur. This is usually accompanied by greater feelings of excitement, and shallow breathing. The body is reacting to the pleasurable stimulation.

Step six. More extensive touching and fondling. This includes 'petting' — touching the girl's breasts outside her clothes, and then to touching genitals outside the clothes.

Step seven. Heavy petting — touching each other's genitals. Obviously this means that both have undressed to some extent. Once this kind of contact is made, it really is hard to stay in control, because the next step becomes very urgent.

Step eight. Mutual masturbation — when you stimulate each other's genitals, maybe to orgasm.

Step nine. Oral sex, also maybe to orgasm. This is also 'simulated sexual intercourse' because it has much the same effect.

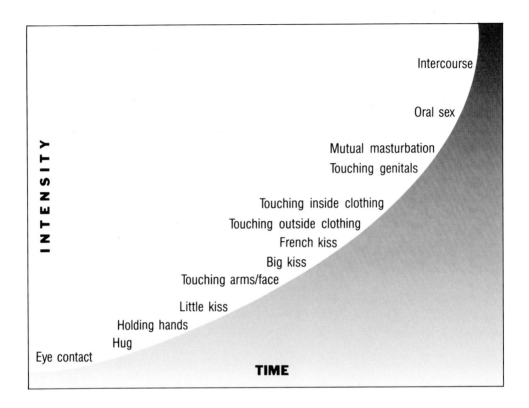

Intercourse

Oral sex

Mutual masturbation
Touching genitals

Touching inside clothing
Touching outside clothing
French kiss
Big kiss
Touching arms/face

Little kiss
Holding hands
Hug
Eye contact

INTENSITY

TIME

Step ten. Sexual intercourse (penetration of the vagina by the penis).

Whatever steps you count (and you can count more or less) the progression is clear. One step leads directly to the next, and unless you recognize what is happening you can easily end up at the top of that ladder.

The Bible doesn't spell out where to draw the line. But it's clear that once genital contact is made it becomes increasingly difficult to deny the urge that leads to full intercourse, or masturbation/oral sex to orgasm. So our counsel is to slow down the steps, and make no rush

to climb the ladder. Avoid long petting sessions when the process can continue further than both of you intend. And to spend hours in 'snorkelling kisses' (you only come up for air!) will not help your self-control, however much fun it may seem at the time.

Sexual intercourse — in case there is some doubt — is when the penis enters the vagina, and the man pushes in and out. This process (thrusting) is aided by lubrication provided by the vagina. At the same time both the man and the woman experience many sensations, body flushes, rapid breathing and so on.

If the clitoris is properly stimulated, the woman may have an orgasm, which is defined as the exciting release of intense pleasure (described by one as the feeling you get when you're about to sneeze!). The man orgasms by ejaculating (shooting semen into the vagina), which is accompanied by a similar release of great pleasure. After this there is a process of recovery and rest. For those not married this can be a time of terrible guilt and fear; so-called 'post-coital depression'. But for those committed to each other this can be a wonderful time of recognizing God's gift of sex that expresses their great love.

God has clearly spelled out that sexual intercourse is to be reserved for marriage. To do 'everything else but' isn't helpful either, since as we've pointed out, oral sex and mutual masturbation are a kind of simulated sex. You want to keep your relationship good and healthy, so make the early steps last!

THE CONSEQUENCES OF SEX

You do need to be aware of the consequences of sex. Because of the pleasures involved, sometimes it's easy to forget. But intercourse is the way God designed that sperm and egg come into contact. So one obvious possible consequence is pregnancy. And the sad fact is that unplanned pregnancies are more likely for those who are Christian. The reason for this is that the unmarried Christian couple have not intended to 'go all the way'. When they do, for whatever reason, they are less likely to have taken precautions. We have seen a number of couples who have fallen into this trap, and it always causes great grief. So don't get fooled.

Then there are the other 'things' that can be transferred at the same time. Later on we'll spend more time

Holding, touching and kissing, is the start of a progression which is designed to bring great pleasure but which is also difficult to stop.

on the hazards of sex. But you need to be doubly aware of the diseases that can kill you, or make life very unpleasant. You're really gambling with your life to have unprotected sex nowadays. That's why you have to be in a relationship that is totally committed — marriage. Why? Because you need to have complete trust, and should something terrible occur, you need to be able to work together and share together, and even support the other in dying. Sex is too dangerous not to have that complete commitment. The answer to avoid AIDS is not in 'safe sex' (which isn't!) but in God's plan for your sexuality.

But even greater than all these terrible consequences is the greatest disaster of all — spiritual death. Sex misused always takes you away from your God. Not because He draws back, but because you will. You cannot have wrong sex and still feel comfortable with the God of truth and right. You will notice your own spirituality decline. And most of all, that's the worst consequence of a sexual life apart from God. God is not against sex. He just wants it to be the best it can be in your life. He wants you to reject the messed-up version of sex the world wants to sell you. So remember the consequences of sex, and make sure you keep it good and right.

For God made you in the first place! 'For you created my inmost being; you knit me together in my mother's womb. I praise you be-

The girl is most likely to bear the consequences of sex without commitment. Instead of being the fulfilment of a relationship pregnancy brings a host of problems.

cause I am fearfully and wonderfully made . . . .' (Psalm 139:13, 14, NIV.) More than just knowing about the physical parts and how they work, *we need an owner's manual* on how to use this complicated mechanism that sometimes seems to try to take control.

GETTING THE RIGHT GEAR

What to compare sex with? How about something that most men are in love with anyway: the car.

But first some reservations. This is not a connection between car mechanics and sex. That would be too basic. What we're talking about is *how* you drive the car, and *how* you look after it. For if you know the principles of safe driving and respect for your vehicle, you'll also know the principles of sexual expression and respect for your body!

First, what do you do? You check all the controls, and make sure you know what everything does. That way you don't get caught out, right! Same with your sexuality. You need to understand it, and how each part works. Don't fall for the old excuse, 'I didn't know what I was doing.'

GET INTO GEAR

Once we've checked the controls, looked in the mirror, then what? You check the gear stick. Because before you can drive, you have to put the engine into the right gear! You've heard about the sex drive — that's the engine that pushes you along. But the gearbox is the mind; the way you control the driving power of the machine that is your sexuality. So let's look at the different gears:

Neutral: We all start here. No one *has* to be sexually active! And there's nothing wrong in doing nothing. Just because the whole world screams at you to have sex doesn't mean you have to comply. And nobody gets hurt in a car that isn't moving (unless someone else hits you, of course!).

First Gear: We can liken this to awareness. You notice girls for the first time as something other than

minor annoyances. You somehow want to get to know them better. And they seem to be so different and hard to understand. This is the beginning of experimentation, the first step on the journey.

Second Gear: This is like the car gathering speed. Not too fast, but there is an acceleration towards intimacy. You're starting to get involved, and making your discoveries. As the speed increases, you find out about kissing and cuddling, about the physical things we've noted above. The relationship is developing.

Third Gear: Here we come to much closer bonding which needs to be accompanied by trust. The intimacy is also at a much higher level, and you know each other pretty well. Physical involvement needs to be strongly limited. And as the revs increase, this leads on to engagement, the intention of marriage.

Fourth gear: Now we reach the fulfilled relationship in which there is total trust and commitment. This means marriage, and full sexual expression in this wonderful union. For many couples this may seem the final stage. But surprisingly, there is another . . . .

Overdrive: This really is 'top gear!' For even within marriage, the relationship grows and deepens, becoming stronger and more interdependent. As this process moves along, we find cruising contentment along the highway of life.

So that's the ideal. Of course, it doesn't always work out that way, sadly. But it's important to keep in mind the stages represented by the gears, and to know where you are. So now let's look at some common problems and see how they can be represented by the same illustration.

THE PROBLEMS

Crashing gears: An obvious mistake but something that happens a lot in sexual activity. Remember you have to move through the gears, and not try to rush things! If you're just learning, you will crash some gears, but learn from your mistakes and don't do it again.

Revving the engine in neutral: Racing the engine without using its power doesn't get you anywhere, nor does it do the engine any good. So, too, firing up your body's sexual chemistry when there's no outlet — or only dangerous ones. To keep on pressing the accelerator only wastes fuel, and gets the engine so hot it starts burning oil. You owe it to yourself and to your girl-friend not to keep on getting excited. One day you might throw the gear lever and you'd be rushing off at breakneck speed that might indeed break your necks. Don't leave yourself 'all revved up and nowhere to go'!

Trying to start in fourth gear: If you've ever tried this on some poor car you'll know that this is not wise. The engine groans and labours, and it tries to get going in jumps and shudders. Just as you wouldn't try to put a car into fourth gear without going through the others first, don't jump into a high level of sexual activity. To rush straight to sex without the steps of intimacy is just like the damage you do to the gearbox and engine by starting in fourth. (Remember the gearbox is your mind, and the engine your sexual drive. You can damage both by such unwise actions.) Damaged synchromesh and a blown engine won't get you very far in life.

Driving in reverse at 80mph: Never tried it? Neither have we! But that's the equivalent of what some do to their sexuality. Going the wrong way very fast. Misdirected sexuality (you can look at this in chapter 8) is dangerous anyway, the more so if it is rushed. Just because some sexual activity seems appealing, don't rush into anything. And don't take your girl on a mad joy-ride down some sexual highway.

Leaving the handbrake on: You've engaged the right gear. You've checked your mirror. You've indicated the way you're going. But as you try to move off, nothing happens. You finally discover you've left the handbrake on. The sexual equivalent is to go right into the way this world says you should act, but still keep one foot on the religious floor. You want to experiment and do things that sound like a lot of fun, but your morals will not let you. So you end up trying to drive with the handbrake on. You can even do this (each of us can confess to doing this) but you burn up the handbrake and strain the engine. Not a clever

For many males the car has become a virility symbol and they drive in a selfish and thoughtless style, similar to their sex lives.

way to treat your car. Not a clever way to treat yourself sexually. And it can be confusing to your girl-friend too, who wonders what's going on. One moment you're throwing yourself at her, the next you panic and run away. You need to work out your sexuality with God, and act responsibly.

Never using the clutch: Rally drivers are supposed to be able to do this. But it's not recommended. The clutch is there to control the gearbox (your mind and its sexuality). Using the clutch gets a smooth gear change, and you don't jump like a kangaroo down the road. So what controls your gearbox? Maybe the clutch is like the work of the Holy Spirit whom we ask to show us the right way to act. With God involved in the process of exploring sex you can turn to Him for help. And though He won't stop you from making your own choices, He does give the best advice. Use the clutch!

Changing gear but never starting the engine: You're out there sitting in the car. You're getting used to the way the controls work. The best way to do this is when it's not moving, of course. And you need that time. But like a child playing with the gear stick but never starting the engine, you wonder why you're not getting anywhere. In the end you need to make a start, and begin the process of discovery. In some ways, no experience can be as dangerous as too much experience — for to become suddenly sexually aware can

lead you off-track too. So begin gently, and get to know girls. This is best done in a group. That way you can become comfortable, and not make too many mistakes.

Forgetting to put oil in the gearbox: Another pointer to the need to involve God. One symbol in the Bible for the Holy Spirit is oil. And this would apply here too. The oil of the Holy Spirit prevents damage, stops you from drying up, and keeps things running smoothly. You need the oil of the Spirit in your mind-gearbox. Without it, you'll soon be grating the cogs, and breaking that very expensive machine God has so wonderfully given you. Keep reading the Bible, stay in touch with God in prayer, and try to make sure your partner does too.

THE SOLUTIONS

Here are some more preventative measures you can take to make sure you're running your 'car' well:

☐ Stop before things get out of control! Know where the brakes are, and be prepared to use them. (Or to use another image, don't wait until there's a fire before you look for the fire escape.)

☐ Know what the drive is, and how it's supposed to be used. Be aware of what's happening around you, like a good driver should. And don't break the speed limit!

☐ Decide where you're going, why, and how fast! Agree with your co-driver too. For even if you sincerely go the wrong route, you will

If you can share a trust in God, can pray and discuss the Bible together it can put the brakes on sexual permissiveness and provide a formula for a rewarding relationship.

sincerely end up in the wrong place.

But sometimes things have already gone too far. So what then? Carry on driving as you have? No: stop, and get re-directed. Remember:

☐ Sex is not everything! Life is more than physical desire. Don't allow current ideas to clog up your mind, so train your mind to think on good things (see Philippians 4:8).

☐ Make sure you're in control. Don't be a back seat driver either! Most of all, remember you do not have to be a slave to your engine. Make your energetic drive work — especially with physical exercise and hard physical labour. That way you will have less time with your engine running idle, and you can feel (tired, but) happy with the result. The Devil finds work . . . .

☐ Don't become preoccupied with sexual thoughts and fantasies. Don't be fooled: to cultivate a world of fantasy is harmful — your mind may eventually transform rooted fantasies into reality. You can't expect your engine to be OK when you're feeding it rocket fuel!

☐ If things are going too far too fast, STOP. REVERSE. GET OUT OF THE SITUATION! Don't play

games with sex, or keep going close to your limit. Driving at the limit has its own penalties. And avoid situations in which you know things could get out of control.

☐ There is a way back. Don't ignore the warning signs. Use the escape lane. Remember God's forgiveness, remember God can recreate you into His image. He invites you to return to emotional and spiritual virginity. You do not have to stay the way you are.

It's dangerous to ignore warning signs — it can be lethal!

PUTTING PASSION IN ITS PLACE

In all of this remember that it's not the physical side that must be dominant. You must be in control of your drive, not the other way round. To be out of control in a car is a terrifying experience. It's the same in life, and if you are just a slave to your passions, then you will never be truly happy.

Just like driving a car, everything can be wonderful at the right time and in the right situation. So now you know about the mechanics of sex, make sure you leave top gear until you're married.

Pushing your sexual accelerator beyond the limit can result in losing control with disastrous consequences.

QUESTIONS AND ANSWERS

I am single and still a virgin, however I love pictures of girls in magazines. Is this normal?

Maybe, but is it helpful? You don't say whether this is a habit you are trying to break, or just something that you've noticed and have avoided. Just because you are single and a virgin doesn't mean you don't experience sexual excitement. But do realize that this can lead you into other problems like masturbating to erotic pictures or the use of pornography. You need to 'guard the windows of the mind' and make sure you don't spend time in concentrating your thoughts on sexual material that will make things worse.

I don't really believe in sex before marriage but I don't trust myself not to do it. What should I do?

We admire your honesty in distrusting yourself. In some situations it is very hard to stick to your beliefs. That's why, to avoid those situations, you need to understand the physical processes we've mentioned, and not allow yourself to be carried away by the heat of the moment — avoid the moments! You also need to have a clear agreement with your girl-friend that you both take the responsibility for saying 'No'. Add to this the vital aspect of involving God in your decision-making. You need to be honest with Him too, and ask for strength to keep your promises. Remember your future

Glamour girl pictures are everywhere, you can't avoid them, so it depends on you how you let them affect you.

THE UN- PROMISE

No, this has nothing to do with the United Nations! The UN-promise is that you promise yourself not to do anything that begins with 'UN-' when you are with a girl:

I will not UN-DO.
I will not UN-FASTEN.
I will not UN-ZIP.
I will not UN-BUTTON.
I will not UN-HOOK.

Keep your mind engaged. Dozy times are dangerous times if you can't control your thoughts.

marriage will be so much better for having taken a firm line now!

My sexual feelings are so strong that I just can't stand it any more. It's like I'm going to die unless I get satisfaction. How can I deal with these feelings?

Go back to the car illustration we used earlier. Are you filling up on bad fuel? Are you revving up your engine when you know you can't go anywhere? What about your fantasies — do you spend a long time indulging them? In most cases of overwhelming feelings, these come because of what has gone into the mind. So stop anything that might be feeding these feelings. And try to re-direct your mind to more healthy activities. The danger times are when you are alone, unoccupied, just dreaming. So get back to your studies, or your work, or some absorbing activity or sport. And go to God for help in dealing with your thoughts. You won't die from not having sex!

MAKING DECISIONS

A popular song from a while ago describes very graphically the verbal fight between a girl and a boy. The boy wants to 'go all the way'. The girl tells him to 'Stop right there!' Before they go any further she wants to know

if he loves her
if he needs her
if he'll never leave her
if he'll make her happy for the rest of her life
if he'll make her his wife
if he'll love her for ever.

His repeated reply: 'Let me sleep on it.' He promises to tell her in the morning (by which time it will obviously be too late). So she demands to know 'right now' and refuses to go any further unless he gives her an answer. So eventually he promises everything, because 'the feeling comes upon him like a tidal wave'. He promises to love her till the end of time. And now, in the song, he says he's praying for the end of time so he can end his time with her!

A clear illustration of what happens in such a sexual relationship. The girl wants security and commitment, she wants eternal love. The boy wants physical satisfaction and so promises anything and everything to get what he wants. And it ends in tears and disillusionment because the basis for sex was never there.

As well as affection a girl wants security and commitment.

SEXUAL LIES

Tick the ones you've heard. It's amazing how common these mistaken ideas are:

- ☐ You can't get a girl pregnant if you have sex standing up.
- ☐ If she has her period, you're safe.
- ☐ A virgin can't get pregnant the first time she has sex.
- ☐ If the girl urinates after sex, she won't get pregnant.
- ☐ If you don't come (ejaculate) inside the girl, she won't get pregnant.
- ☐ If you use contraception most of the time, you won't get her pregnant.
- ☐ If you don't have sex, you're probably gay.
- ☐ If you don't like the idea of having sex, then you're either impotent or frigid.
- ☐ More sexual experience means a better marriage.
- ☐ Sex shows you really do love each other.
- ☐ If you're engaged, then sex is expected.
- ☐ You don't catch sexual diseases if you're young.
- ☐ Boys need sex more than girls.
- ☐ Girls are made to say no.
- ☐ Men are animals who only want one thing.
- ☐ Once a girl undresses she has to go through with it.
- ☐ Foreplay doesn't mean you'll end up having sex, so do as much as you want.
- ☐ Girls say 'No' when they mean 'Yes'.
- ☐ Sexual involvement can't be reduced, it always increases.
- ☐ Girls use sex to get love, boys use love to get sex.

4

So what's it all about?

Love is patient, love is kind. It does not envy, it does not boast, it is not proud. It is not rude, it is not self-seeking, it is not easily angered, it keeps no record of wrongs. Love does not delight in evil but rejoices with the truth. 1 Corinthians 13:4-6, NIV.

WHAT'S LOVE GOT TO DO WITH IT?

'Love — I don't know. What really scares me is that I'm not sure if I can love. Not really. Not actually love somebody.'

The words of a guy of just 16. Already he's feeling worried that life is passing him by. He sees his friends falling in and out of love (or so they say) and he wonders what's the matter with him. Because all the feelings he gets told about somehow don't seem to happen to *him*.

'I wish I could find someone to love.' Echoed in songs and poetry, in half-heard conversations and problem pages. If 'Love is all around' why can't I find any? If 'All you need is love' why doesn't someone meet my need? Better to have loved and lost than never to have loved at all?

He had such strong feelings, but no way of showing them. A common experience for most teenagers

— the hormones are busy rushing round your body, but you can't find the right person to give all that 'love' to!

And it is confusing. You feel attractions. You find a girl appealing. She seems charming. But then there are all the hurdles to cross before you can even approach her and find out if there are any mutual feelings. And you're still struggling with what love really means.

So many have asked us to tell them whether they are 'in love'. Trouble is, though we can ask some helpful questions, we can't actually *know*. And even more difficult is that often-asked question: 'How can I make her love me?'

Because the truth is that the experience is not transferable. You cannot convey the sensations, thoughts, the all-consuming passion that is love. You can describe love, you can illustrate love, you can show love. But you cannot make anyone else

love, despite all the supposed love potions and aphrodisiacs of the ages.

(And interestingly love is that one thing ultimately of essential value, above all to God, the God of love. Does God demand love? Does He force us? More of that later.)

How to love, how to develop love in others, how to find the true love of life — those are the questions we all face deep down.

What to say to the boy who came and spoke to us. How to ease the anxiety of someone who fears they *cannot* love?

Too much pressure, too many demands, and yet too few answers. All those feelings confused by distorted views of what real love is (and how tragic to even have to say 'real love' — for the word 'love' should be enough. But in this time in which we live, it surely is not enough just to use the word 'love' which has become so empty of real meaning).

Examples? Take just a few foolish thoughts:

LOVE DEFINITIONS

'Love means never having to say you're sorry.' Really? Does that mean as husband and wife we never have to apologize to each other? Or that we never make mistakes? A great way of setting people up for false expectations!

'Love is like the measles; we all have to go through it.' Yes, love may have qualities that throw your world upside-down. Yes, love is disturbing and challenging. But to picture it at the level of some emotional disease is to warp the reality of total commitment and reasonableness that is at the heart of true love. And to suggest it is something that simply has to be endured takes away from the specialness of this great gift.

'Love is blind.' So go into it with your eyes closed, right? Wrong. If you ever needed to be clear-sighted, it's when you love! All those faults you wanted to disregard will have to be dealt with, sometime, someplace. Happiness is not ignorance, intentional or otherwise.

From all the trite sayings to the supposed scientific. How about this for a supposed definition?: 'Love: the cognitive affective state characterized by intrusive and obsessive fantasizing concerning reciprocity of amorant feelings by the object of the amorance.'

Of course! Well, why didn't you say so before?! Such 'explanations' end up confusing and baffling those who are earnestly searching for real answers. And the popular culture hardly helps:

'Love hurts, love scars, love wounds, and mars . . . .' The words of songwriter Boudleaux Bryant sum up the (for some) terrifying experience of love. Negative experiences of love seem to be the universal language of today. With 150,000 divorces in Britain every year (1,177,000 in the US), then perhaps it's true.

The problem with love in most

people's minds is that they have never bothered to discover what it really is. So they go along with the foolish ideas which can make love mean just about anything:

LOVE IS . . .

A hole in the heart.
BEN HECHT

A grave mental disease.
PLATO

A mutual misunderstanding.
OSCAR WILDE

The state in which a man sees things most decidedly as they are not.
FRIEDRICH W. NIETZSCHE

Desperate madness.
JOHN FORD

Just another four-letter word.
TENNESSEE WILLIAMS

Two minds without a single thought.
PHILIP BARRY

The drug which makes sexuality palatable in popular mythology.
GERMAINE GREER

Sentimental measles.
CHARLES KINGSLEY

Love? The real thing isn't slushy sentiment but a principle illustrated by care, commitment and unselfish attitudes.

What has this got to do with the God of love? Not a lot, from what most of the world says. But we must not give up on love just because so many have misunderstood love, or have not recognized what love really is. Why? Because human love is an expression of the love from God, the God of love:

'Whoever loves is a child of God and knows God. Whoever does not love does not know God, for God is love.' (1 John 4:7, 8.) As the Bible so clearly shows us, especially when it tells us that 'God is love,' love is not some kind of funny feeling you get, but a whole principle of life and how to live it.

See why love is so important?

And what *kind* of love is determined by how you define it and how you express it. There is love for brothers and sisters, for fathers and mothers, for friends and neighbours, even for your dog and cat or your favourite food!

But when you read 1 Corinthians 13 you see that the love the Bible is talking about is to do with the way we live. Let us remind you again:

'Love is patient and kind; it is not jealous or conceited or proud; love is not ill-mannered or selfish or irritable; love does not keep a record of wrongs; love is not happy with evil, but is happy with the truth. Love never gives up; and its faith, hope, and patience never fail.' 1 Corinthians 13:4-7.

How does your love measure up? In this kind of love we are reflecting the divine ideal — and the best kind of love is closest to this description of love as a principle which determines our very lives. (For more on this, take a look at the 'Love Test' to see how you view love and how this compares with the right and wrong views of love.)

LOVE AND SEX

Sexual arousal must not be confused with love. Often when sexual arousal happens with a particular person, this is immediately identified as love. Especially if this is the first time, and is mutual, such sexual arousal may be made the basis for saying, 'I am in love.'

LOVE TEST

Love wants to give. Lust wants to take. What do you want?

Love means you also like. Do you really like each other?

What about God? Is He involved in your relationship?

Are you good friends as well as everything else?

Do you trust each other — even with your most intimate secrets?

Love is unselfish. Lust is selfish. What are you?

Are you able to laugh and share fun together?

When you have fights, can you work out your differences?

Can you talk about everything and anything together?

Are you *both* in love — not just one of you?

Love is wise. Infatuation is foolish. Which are you?

Do you believe your relationship will last?

Such confusion of sexual arousal and excitement with love can lead to disastrous consequences. When the 'chemistry' fades, and reality hits, the mistakes may already have been made. Commitment in love cannot be based on the feelings of the moment, however powerful.

Both love and sexual drive are powerful influences on us, but they are not identical. In combination they are God's designed way of showing total commitment and unselfish giving. It is *God's intention* that such love between a man and a woman should be demonstrated in complete sexual union. But to split love and sex apart destroys the divine system of human intimate relationships.

So to indulge in physical sex without love means a selfish satisfaction of sensual desire. To say, in effect, 'I like you so let's have sex' is to exploit the other's whole being in the most intimate way without being willing to give selflessly of your own inner being — which is what love is all about. Truly safe sex is only in love, for love never seeks its own way, never exploits, never imposes its own will. You can only be safe in sex if love is really present, for love will never hurt the object of love.

That's not to say that couples who are truly in love don't make mistakes! But at least this idea avoids the treatment of others as things to be used, as objects of desire to satisfy your physical needs. Seen this way, a woman is just an aid to masturbation, to achieving your own pleasure.

So what if you are both in love. What then? Isn't it OK to do what you want as long as you're in love?

Hardly a safe attitude either, especially if love comes and goes as often as the wind changes direction. Love is far more than a passing attraction, a vision of feminine beauty that happens to pass by making you exclaim, 'I'm in love!'

SEXUAL PROGRESSION

When it comes to a boy-girl relationship, physical contact — whether you call it necking or petting or making out or whatever — must be seen for what it truly is: a preparation for intercourse. Now that may not be on your mind, nor on your girl-friend's. But that is what the mutual touching and excitement of each other's bodies is intended to do. So don't play dumb and end up confessing, 'I didn't know what I was doing', as all too many have told us!

From the first touch there is an unbroken line of physical expression that leads to intercourse. That doesn't mean you have no choice and that your body just takes over. But you need to see that truly 'one thing leads to another'.

The usual first point of contact is holding hands. In our society shaking hands is the formalized way of greeting each other and is not seen as meaning anything more than that. But once the hand is held longer, or touched in different ways, then this can become a sexual expression. Caresses, lingering touches, extended contact — even hands are 'sexual organs'!

This leads to touching other parts of the body, usually first the arms and back, then moving on to legs, front and face. At the same time kissing begins and becomes more 'passionate' — which in turn leads to 'French kissing' (insertion of tongue), and so on.

Then follows what is normally termed petting — the touch of the girls breasts and the genital area outside her clothes — and then heavy petting (direct contact with these areas inside her clothes). Beyond this is mutual stimulation of the genitals and intercourse.

One step leads almost inexorably to the other, unless certain decisions have been clearly made beforehand. It is possible to stop at any point, but once genital contact is reached this may prove increasingly difficult, which is why many Christian counsellors recommend that any petting stops well before this.

It is normal and natural to want to express your love physically. To suggest that you should not kiss until marriage is ridiculous, and a rule that will either be broken and lead to guilt and worse, or will prevent a good relationship ever being developed. But what you *must* decide is what you really want. And I mean *really want*. Your sex drive may be urging you towards sexual intercourse or some kind of 'satisfaction', but is that what you most desire? These kinds of decisions must be made before you arrive at the critical point, and you should have discussed them with your girlfriend too. Knowing where both of you are going to draw the line will be important and helpful to you in your close relationship.

Knowing that going too far in physical terms will cause you much sadness and heartbreak can help you mentally to decide what level of physical contact is acceptable. You may choose simply to kiss and touch, without making contact with the sexual areas (breasts and genitals). At least you have both mentally decided.

But simply to rely on your own mental decisions is not enough. You must also plan ahead so that you will not place yourselves in positions which will be tempting and difficult. In the same way as someone giving up smoking throws out their cigarettes, keep yourselves away from long periods of being alone together, especially late at night. Your best decisions may be difficult to maintain in an atmosphere of closeness and togetherness when you're half asleep!

AM I IN LOVE?

That's a question we often get asked. Couples come along and ask if we can tell — as if we have a magic 'love-ometer' that can measure love! You may have feelings that you think may be love, but you're not sure. And even if you are 'in love', is this the person you should marry?

So how can you tell?

Firstly, love is not blind, whatever people say. If you are deliberately ignoring things about your partner, then you are being foolish. And if you are trying to build up a false image, then this can also cause 'love-confusion'. Why? Because to love someone means to accept them as they are, not the image we have of them in our minds.

Then remember the qualities that define love. Love means acceptance, responsibility, respect, loyalty, honesty, trust, truthfulness and so on. Love is not a quick thrill of physical sex. Love can be made cheap and unpleasant. Love is not just a feeling. It is a way of living — a principle.

So what do you mean when you tell a girl 'I love you'?

Do you mean: 'I want to sleep with you'?

Or, 'I like you a lot'?

Or, 'I want more from you'?

Or, 'I want to marry you'?

Or, 'I respect, value, adore, trust, accept . . . you'?

Love means many things to different people. And you need to explain what you mean. And you certainly must never use 'I love you' as a way of forcing someone, or getting your own way.

Love has no strings. You cannot say, 'I will love you if you do as I

Unless you can agree on the direction your lives should go even though you have many similarities in character, likes and dislikes, it could all fall apart.

say.' Or, 'I will love you if you give me sex.' Or, 'I will love you if you will give up your career.' That is selfishness, not love. Nor can you love just because the other person is or has something you want (beauty, money, possessions or power).

Love is given without expecting something in return. That is God's love, as shown in Jesus, totally unselfish and committed.

MAKING THE RIGHT CHOICE

Can you choose who to love?

Maybe you should have a list of all the qualities the right girl needs to have?

Or should you rush off and marry the first person you have some odd feelings for?

No to all three questions! But you do need to think seriously as you choose the person you intend to spend your whole life with. You can't leave it to chance, or to some funny feelings (which could be due to eating some bad food or something!). We suggest you set some guidelines to help yourself.

And while this does not guarantee a happy and fulfilled relationship, we do believe you should agree on the fundamentals of life. That includes meaning and purpose, goals and ideals — and, most essentially, your beliefs about God and His involvement in your lives. If you cannot agree on this, then it will be very hard to work through all the problems that will be caused. That's why the Bible talks about being unequally yoked (2 Cor. 6:14), and can two walk together except they be agreed (see Amos 3:3).

In fact, if this basic fundamental

GOING OUT

A Yes/No quiz for you on the who, what and when of getting friendly.

Y N

- ☐ ☐ I prefer to go out with a group rather than be alone with a girl.
- ☐ ☐ I like to meet the girl's parents before going out with a her.
- ☐ ☐ I try at least to get a kiss the first time I go out with a girl.
- ☐ ☐ I respect a girl more who is clear that she isn't going to have sex.
- ☐ ☐ I rely on the girl to say no.
- ☐ ☐ I like to do other things than just be romantic when I go with someone.
- ☐ ☐ I try to avoid getting into difficult situations.
- ☐ ☐ I make sure we both know where we're going beforehand.
- ☐ ☐ I'm not affected by the way the girl dresses.
- ☐ ☐ I always make sure I get home at a reasonable time.

If only the choice was this simple! But then it depends on your reasons for choosing. Looks yes, but goals, ideals, character and an active belief in God are essential elements in a successful partnership.

is solid and real, then just about everything else that may come between you can be resolved — because you have God there in the middle of the relationship. Even so, it's wise to consider factors of age, race, background, culture, language and so on. Take a look at 'Who Should I Choose' on the next page. And although you shouldn't make such a definite list, it's helpful to think about what is important to you.

MAKING YOUR CHOICE

Examine some of these ideas and circle those that you believe are significant:

caring	sure of herself
gentle	honest
looks a real beauty	likes what I like
lives what she believes	dependable
clever	hard-worker
considerate towards others	forgiving
reliable	doesn't give up easily
forceful	attractive
good sense of humour	funny
sexy	good listener
good-looking	communicates well
looks after herself	popular
well-dressed	talented
patient	has money
a Christian	even-tempered
	quiet
	ambitious

And there may be others that occur to you. Remember, you're not writing out a recipe, just getting clear in your mind what you think is important.

This is particularly important in those societies where others are also involved in the decision-making process. Good parents will want their children to be happy, and not force them to marry someone who will not be compatible. So there needs to be a long process of getting to know each other before final decisions are arrived at.

The choices are for you and your future wife. We cannot tell you if you are making the right choices. Even Christian marriages break up. But by making sure you have talked about the fundamentals of life, agreeing on your religious convictions, and truly loving and admiring each other — you will have a much greater chance of success. And please remember that beauty is not to be the most important factor, for beauty fades, and is no guarantee of a good character!

The basis of a truly Christian marriage is the trust and certainty that comes from knowing each other as a child of God. If you are both convinced of the importance of following God's way, of truly loving and forgiving each other, then smile and be happy in the Lord. We have found this to be the secret of our happy marriage of more than twenty years; we wish the same for you.

WHO SHOULD I CHOOSE?

There seem to be so many opinions about the 'right' girl. How do you make up your mind? Most of all, what qualities are important in making your choice?

The obvious reasons are to do with *externals*; how she looks. Is she beautiful? Does she have a good figure? Do you find her physically attractive? Add to this the way she dresses, her possessions, where she lives, her family background, wealth, status. What about her abilities? Can she cook, clean, work hard? Some just seem to be looking for a beast of burden!

Then there's her behaviour. What does this say about her? Is she happy, friendly, flirtatious, angry, hostile, caring, approachable, cold or what?

But like God we as Christians need to be less concerned with the outward appearance. God looks at the heart, and we must try to follow this approach. We are not to be so concerned with the way society chooses, but look for the true qualities of character.

So how? God has given us some excellent principles.

The Bible has much to say about the *kind* of people Christians are to be, and the importance of not being bound to 'unbelievers' (2 Corinthians 6:14-16). While some may try to do 'romance evangelism', the general result is that the Christian is led astray, not that the non-Christian is converted. So while it's important to

If you have niggling doubts about a relationship don't be too proud to ask for advice from someone you trust. And be prepared to listen even if it's not what you want to hear!

question will always be there, 'Did he/she do that just because of me?'

God is not silent. He does not control who we go out with, but He is most definitely interested. So pray about it, and the more you seem to be falling in love, the more you should be praying. Don't ask God to confirm what you have already decided. Be honest and open, whatever you may feel for someone. And pray *now* before you get involved — so that you are prepared. All too often we wait until we are hopelessly in love and then hope God will approve.

Ask other Christians who have had good life-experience. You can get an objective view from someone who cares about you and who can see the situation — maybe more clearly than you can! Be careful who you confide in, but if you can find someone to trust, then their advice may be very helpful.

Talk to your parents. Of course they're biased! But they still want the best for you, and they have invested much time and trouble in you! They will certainly appreciate your maturity in talking together about such important matters.

Don't rush! Going out with a girl is not an Olympic event! You can afford to take your time. So keep a cool head and enjoy the process of discovery — of yourself as well as the girl. Most importantly don't let the physical rush ahead of the mental, emotional and spiritual relationship.

make friends of non-Christians, it can be very damaging and dangerous to become involved with a non-Christian partner. Also, should the non-Christian accept Jesus, the

QUESTIONS AND ANSWERS

What about dating or going out together? What should we do?

A good question — because what is usually asked is, 'What shouldn't we do?' We would suggest that you do things not just as a couple, but with other friends. And if you do go out on a date, think of some fun activity like a sport you can both play, or make a meal together and so on. Just normal things like decorating a room can be fun when it's done together. What isn't helpful is time spent kissing and cuddling in a car or alone in a room. That's not to say you're not trustworthy, just that we all know how our physical feelings can carry us away. So concentrate on sharing in some innocent activities.

I'm desperately in love with a girl. How do I know if this is what God wills?

Not by deciding for yourself! All too often we decide what God's will is, and then tell Him what we've decided. You need to spend time together with the girl (we presume you've told her!) and see whether you share the same feelings, goals, and fundamental beliefs. And through prayer and the way God leads, we believe that marriage will be as natural as it was for us.

What about love at first sight?

This is often given as a reason for a quick courtship or for a rush to become intimate. While it may be true that instant attraction can occur, this doesn't mean it's love. If we fell in love with everyone we were attracted to, then . . . ! Looking back, you may think of the first occasion when you met, and it may seem that love began then. But love is a principle, not a feeling that comes from a look. You can hardly be in love with someone you've just seen, or only had a brief conversation with. Love means trust and commitment, and this can only be when you know each other well.

What's the difference between love and sex?

A sad question, if it's true. Because you should already recognize many kinds of love — for your family, for your friends generally, and for God. If you are trying to separate love from sex in a current relationship with a girl, you need to do some serious thinking. Sex is an important part of a love relationship between husband and wife, and the beginning of this comes during the courtship process — with kissing and cuddling, etc. But it is just one aspect of love, physical and spiritual. Don't make sex equal to love, or the other way round. Love is a principle for living, sex is one physical part of that love that is special in marriage. So don't be fooled by those who see no difference. There's all the difference in the world between a few minutes 'fun' and a lifetime of trust and assurance.

Pressure to find a partner has meant many starting to conform much earlier in their lives!

When should you start going out with girls?

We don't think this should be such an important question if you have already developed a good social group that includes girls. The problem today is that there is pressure to go out together, and more and more encouragement for girl-friends and boy-friends at a very early age. We believe this is an unhealthy development. Certainly to become intimate with a girl should not be the intention anyway. Thirteen and 14 (and even earlier) is surely too early to begin the process of sexual experimentation. Even the State doesn't recognize sexual relationships before the age of 16. But we sadly observe that many do begin very young, and would appeal for great caution. Make sure you make extending your circle of friends more of a priority than spending time alone with one girl. And don't rush — you have a whole lifetime to live!

I'm not so young any more and feel I should find someone to marry quickly. It's not that I'm desperate, but I don't think I should wait too long. What do you think?

Don't start rushing around trying to find a girl just because of this. It's a terrible reason for marriage, and could lead to disaster. Like any love relationship, it needs to be based on mutual love and trust, not because you feel time is running out! 'Marry in haste, repent at leisure' is a proverb that contains much truth!

Is it OK to date someone who isn't a Christian?

A common question. It depends on what you really mean. From what we've said so far it's clear that you need to be looking for someone who shares the same spiritual values you have. So if there's no common ground, there's little point in developing a serious relationship. But there's nothing wrong in becoming friendly with others outside the Church. They need to see Christians and how they behave; you have a witness to give. But from our experience, most relationships leading to marriage between Christians and non-Christians are not happy, and cause too many problems.

5

Don't believe all you hear!

Be on your guard, and do not let anyone deceive you. Matthew 24:4. Test everything. Hold on to the good. Avoid every kind of evil. 1 Thessalonians 5:21, 22, NIV.

SEX PRESSURE

'Everybody's doing it' is what we're told so often. In discussion with teens it is assumed that sex is commonplace. Sexual activity is a fact of life for the vast majority, 'so why should I be any different?' comes the question.

We need to admit there's a great deal of pressure for premarital sex — even for young teenagers. Now nobody can say that society 'made' them have sex, but since it is so 'permissible' today, then the pressure can be hard to resist. Especially when you have no reason to say 'No' or have any moral principles.

The movies say it's fun. The magazines say it's wonderful. Your friends say it's great. What do you do? Believe everyone else is wrong?

Hard, isn't it? But you need to know that the idea that 'Everybody's doing it' is a lie. And more of your friends than you think are not telling the truth either. Even if the whole world is doing it, then you don't need to follow right along.

If you don't have sex you're not odd, or strange, or peculiar. On the contrary, you are being wise, responsible, and truly caring. For just because so many do foolishly have wrong sex doesn't turn wrong into right. And it's wrong because such sex wounds and destroys, hurts and even kills. Which is why God says it's wrong.

So we need to look at some of these lies and expose them for what they really are.

SEX FICTION

LIE 1. **Sex is what you need for a happy life**

Sex in the right place at the right time with the right person (your wife!) can make life marvellously happy. But sex is not a great cure-all for unhappiness. In fact, there's probably more unhappiness caused by wrong sex than any one other single factor. A moment's pleasure, a lifetime's grief. Is that worthwhile? Sex can only be truly happy as part of a loving, committed relationship between a man and a woman — two now one — who have given themselves to each other totally before God.

LIE 2. **Sex will cure your problems**

Sex can never solve your problems, especially when it's wrongly used. Sex is no magic pill to make you forget all your sorrows. More than likely, use sex wrongly and it will give you many more problems and really complicate your life. If you have relationship problems, to use sex to fix them will surely make them worse. That's not just a moral argument, we have seen this happen time and again in actual experience. Believe us!

LIE 3. **What you do with sex is up to you, and you alone**

Oh, really? We thought sex usually involved two people! So what about your partner in all of this? Doesn't she have a say in the matter? And what about the effect your sexual behaviour has on others. What about the transmission of diseases — something that involves us all. And what about possible pregnancy — isn't someone else involved there too? You may think it's up to you, but even the values and decisions you make are affected by other people. While sex needs to be kept private, you have a bigger responsibility than just thinking of yourself.

LIE 4. **Sex is just physical pleasure**

No it isn't! Sex is far more than that! The physical part is meant to be the tip of the emotional, mental and spiritual iceberg. If you limit sex to physical pleasure then it's deficient and inadequate. We'd even say that purely physical sex isn't true sex at all, for it's missing the vital aspects of a deep spiritual relationship. Sex as a physical act is just satisfying a need like eating for hunger and drinking for thirst, and, as such, has no great worth or meaning.

You can turn your back on your past but casual sex can leave casualties in its wake.

LIE 5. **A real love-relationship must include sex**

Not if it's really love — until you're really sure. And being really sure is the other side of the marriage service! Think of how many couples split up, even when engaged. And brides and bridegrooms jilted at the altar . . . . Real love waits. For the man who thinks of his future wife before himself wants to make sex the best gift. So to make it part of a relationship before is like giving your money away before you're sure about what you're buying. Very foolish, and may cost you a great deal in the long term. And remember, sex is the highest form of gift you can give of yourself in love. So keep the best till last.

LIE 6. **Sex is for good and won't hurt you**

Yes, God did make sex, and like everything else God created He made it good. Even 'very good'! But why did He give such clear advice as to the right use of this gift? Why did we give such clear instructions to our son when we gave him his first penknife? Because while a penknife rightly used is a great tool and very useful for a multitude of jobs, wrongly used it can cut and hurt and do considerable damage. So with sex; it can really hurt you and others, even though it was designed for good. For like anything else, it can be used or abused, for good or for evil. So don't be fooled, you can get badly hurt through sex.

WHAT I BELIEVE

Ten statements that reveal your beliefs about sex.

YES NO

☐ ☐ Experimenting is the best way to find out about sex.

☐ ☐ Sex is nobody else's business but mine.

☐ ☐ The Church is out of date when it comes to sex.

☐ ☐ Sex is best kept until marriage.

☐ ☐ I don't know much about sex.

☐ ☐ You can do everything except have intercourse.

☐ ☐ Being in love means having sex.

☐ ☐ The Bible is against sex generally.

☐ ☐ All kinds of sex are fine as long as you both are happy.

☐ ☐ Sex is really important to me.

LIE 7. **Sex is for having fun**

As if sex is just another kind of entertainment; like TV or a funfair or any other kind of 'amusement'. Yes, sex can be great fun. But it's not a toy or a computer game or a rollercoaster ride. Sex has very serious consequences, and mustn't be treated so casually.

LIE 8. **Sex is the most wonderful experience**

Yes, this is a lie! Because it is used in situations where sex is wrong. Sex *can* be the most wonderful experience, but that shouldn't tempt you to try it out now. You need to be 'one' emotionally, mentally and spiritually before you make yourself 'one' physically. You need to grow together first, you need to develop your relationship so it is healthy and good. Otherwise sex can be the worst experience and drive the two of you apart. And remember that the female sexual response needs more time, so a quick coupling that satisfies your demands will leave her feeling cheated. And in the end you cheat yourself of something wonderful too. Don't waste the gift!

> **'It is not too much to say that we are living in an age of collective sexual obsession.'**
> ROBERT GRIMM

MAKING IT PLAIN

So often sex is shown as something that 'isn't that bad' or 'doesn't matter much'. But for the Christian, wrong sex will always be wrong. We need to remind ourselves of the very definite position the Bible takes on the matter of the

SEX: Where I get my ideas from

My ideas about sex come from:	Mostly	Some	Occasionally	Never
My parents				
My friends				
Books/magazines				
Films/TV				
Pop music				
Teachers				
The Church				

wrong use of our sexual gifts.

'What human nature does is quite plain. It shows itself in immoral, filthy, and indecent actions.' (Galatians 5:19.)

No debate here! Our human nature is related to our immoral actions. So we cannot say that immorality is acceptable in any way. Instead the Scriptures tell us to:

'Avoid immorality. . . . Don't you know that your body is the temple of the Holy Spirit, who lives in you and who was given to you by God? You do not belong to yourselves but to God.' (1 Corinthians 6:18, 19.)

And so the clear advice is given:

'Do not give in to bodily passions, which are always at war against the soul.' (1 Peter 2:11.)

Why? Because of the terrible consequences of sexual evil that results in so much pain and suffering. Rather 'God wants you to be holy and completely free from sexual immorality.' (1 Thessalonians 4:3.)

That's the only safe way to live. For many today this is 'a hard saying' as the disciples once said to Jesus. But the more we study this question, the more we're convinced of its truth.

For to live a life dominated by sexual passion means you will never be free, never able to be the person God wants you to be. For lust blinds the eye, and prevents deep and profound relationships. Living this way means not knowing God:

'Each of you men should know how to live with his wife in a holy and honourable way, not with lustful desire, like the heathen who do not know God.' (1 Thessalonians 4:4.)

And we need to repeat here: this is not because God is against sex. He just knows how powerful this drive can be, and so He wants it to be channelled into the most meaningful of relationships.

ON MAKING DECISIONS

So how do you decide what to do, sexually? Who do you listen to? What values do you have? What principles do you use? Take a look at this story, and realize that human nature hasn't changed much for thousands of years:

'Once I was looking out of the window of my house, and I saw many inexperienced young men, but noticed one foolish fellow in particular. He was walking along the street near the corner where a certain woman lived. He was passing near her house in the evening after it was dark. And then she met him; she was dressed like a prostitute and was making plans. She was a bold and shameless woman who always walked the street or stood waiting at a corner, sometimes in the streets, sometimes in the market place. She threw her arms around the young man, kissed him, looked him straight in the eye, and said, ''I made my offerings today and have the meat from the sacrifices. So I came out looking for you. I wanted to find you, and here you are! I've covered my bed with sheets of coloured linen from Egypt. I've perfumed it with myrrh, aloes, and cinnamon. Come on! Let's make love all night long. We'll be happy in each other's arms. My husband isn't at home. He's gone away on a long journey. He took plenty of money with him and won't be back for two weeks.''

'So she tempted him with her charms, and he gave in to her smooth talk. Suddenly he was going with her like an ox on the way to be slaughtered, like a deer prancing into a trap where an arrow would pierce its heart. He was like a bird going into a net — he did not know that his life was in danger.

'Now then, sons, listen to me. Pay attention to what I say. Do not let such a woman win your heart; don't go wandering after her. She has been the ruin of many men and caused the death of too many to count. If you go to her house, you are on the way to the world of the dead. It is a short cut to death.' (Proverbs 7:6-27.)

These words were written nearly 3,000 years ago! Doesn't that tell you something about sexual temptation and the disaster that always follows? Listen to what Solomon is saying. Remember, he's speaking from bitter experience. And don't fall into the same trap. His best advice: 'Treat wisdom as your sister, and insight as your closest friend. They will keep you away from other men's wives, from women with seductive words.' (Proverbs 7:4, 5.)

ONCE UPON A TIME

We heard the following story firsthand, and know it to be true. It reflects so many of the current ideas about sex that we believe it is worth repeating here. This is what we were told:

'Jim was an intelligent man. But he had been fooled by all the sexual images around him, taken in by the religion of sex. One day he was working something out on his calculator. I asked him what he was doing.

'"Oh," he said. "Just calculating the number of times I've had sex."

'I must have looked surprised, because he grinned, and then did another calculation. "And that's the number of women I've had sex with!"

'He looked so pleased with himself, as if waiting for me to say "Congratulations".

'I told him I didn't think that was a good way to live. He strongly disagreed, and told me I didn't know what I was missing. He went

> If I love my wife, if I accept marriage as an institution of God, then there comes an inner freedom and certainty of life and action in marriage; I no longer watch with suspicion every step that I take; I no longer call into question every deed that I perform.
>
> DIETRICH BONHOEFFER

Making personal decisions that contradict the trendy ideas of your peers or friends may mean being looked upon as odd and out of touch.

> **Love is so misused a word. I don't even know what it means, do you? What is it: compassion, *caritas*, pity? In any case, it has nothing to do with lust, and the mixing up of the two is one of the reasons we're in such trouble emotionally.**
>
> GORE VIDAL

It's objectionable to live a life-style that results in women being treated as objects rather than as equals in partnership.

on to describe his wife-swapping, his 'fun times' with three in a bed, and all kinds of sexual activities. I shook my head, and told him my marriage was better than all of that! And I warned him that he was being incredibly foolish. He just laughed and walked off.

'Three weeks after that conversation, he came to me in despair. "My wife's gone off with my best friend. It happened last weekend, after we swapped again. And she's taking the kids, and I'm left with nothing." His life came crashing down around him, leaving him dazed and desperate. It took many long walks around the car park to calm him down.

'He experienced the truth that the preachers of today's sex religion don't tell you — the agony of marital breakdown, the burden of guilt, the total failure that makes you want to kill yourself.

'Soon after that I left. I didn't see him for several years until I ran into him in the street. With someone else, who was not his wife, nor his wife-swap partner of before, nor (so I found out later) the next. Just another in the long line of women in his life. He hadn't learnt, and so he'd just kept on going around in circles, following the futile religion of pointless sex. But he certainly wasn't happy.'

SEXUAL SELFISHNESS

He lived a sex-life without understanding the basic principle of love, which is self-giving. Since sex must always be part of this love, it must have the same character — patient, unselfish, truthful.

True sexual expression is not just concerned with following the foolish ideas around today. It's not pleasing yourself. It's being true to yourself and being right, even if all around you are going wrong!

You need to see that there are two

totally different ways of living set before you. Sex as selfishness is the way of the world; and so is the 'prove yourself a man' idea. How can you value a real relationship with a real woman if you follow such thoughts? In so many ways, today's views are opposed to God's intention for sex, opposed to marriage itself.

Mutual trust is so essential to a happy married relationship. How can you have this kind of trust if you view women as objects to be used, as tools for pleasure or whatever? If sex is selfish, it can only be wrong. Don't mix up love and lust. Love means self-giving, of thinking of the other person before yourself. So ask yourself: Where are you in your thinking? Do you still believe everything you hear?

SEX: So who's telling the truth?

This multiple choice questionnaire is to help you see the great difference between the attitudes of modern society and Christian values. You need to decide who's telling the truth!

Sex before marriage is OK
- ☐ when no one can see what you're doing
- ☐ whenever
- ☐ if you feel like it
- ☐ never
- ☐ if you're in love

What do you do when you feel tempted to have sex?
- ☐ give in
- ☐ see how long you can stand the temptation
- ☐ take a cold shower
- ☐ pray about it
- ☐ run as far from the temptation as possible

If someone makes a sexual joke, do you
- ☐ laugh loudly
- ☐ look the other way
- ☐ tell one too
- ☐ leave the conversation
- ☐ tell them it's disgusting

Sexual sin is wrong because
- ☐ there's no such thing as sexual sin
- ☐ your girl-friend might get pregnant
- ☐ God says so
- ☐ you can damage yourself emotionally and spiritually
- ☐ you can get AIDS

Sex is supposed to be enjoyed
- ☐ by anyone
- ☐ only if you're married
- ☐ even if you're just engaged
- ☐ if you and your girl-friend want to
- ☐ sex is not supposed to be enjoyed

QUESTIONS AND ANSWERS

Why is there so much nonsense talked about sex? Why don't people just tell the truth?

Good questions! But there's always the problem of how we look to other people. That's why some boys want to 'act macho' and show off to other boys, and especially look good for the girls. So it's often hard to get at the truth. Added to that is the fact that this world doesn't want to be particularly moral and responsible. So many people talk up sex, saying that it's so much fun and can solve your problems. What they don't tell you is the down-side, of diseases and unwanted pregnancies and self-disgust.

I have played around a bit with sex but even though it was fun at the time I feel bad now. What should I do?

Get out of whatever sexual activity you're involved with, and make sure your sex principles are true and healthy. Like so many, you have probably fallen for the sex lies that are told today. You need to go back and take a long, hard look at your life, and what part sex should play in it. And realize that this world doesn't have your best interests at heart.

How can I avoid getting fooled sexually?

You don't say whether you mean fooled by some particular temptation or the whole world-view about sex. The answer to both is to make sure your sexual *principles* are right (you get these from the Bible) and that your *practices* are healthy. God can help you since what we're talking about is sexual temptation. This is like any desire to sin; victory comes only through God's changing of your whole life. As He remakes us in His image, then temptations begin to lose their force through the strength God gives.

I really don't see what's wrong with sex.

A statement more than a question. But behind it lies the thought that today's views of sex are OK. 'Why get so worried about it?' as one teenager once asked us. For a more complete answer you'll need to go back and read this whole chapter. But in brief, what's wrong with many of today's ideas of sex is that a person thinks only of himself, and of the physical part of sexuality. If you can't see what's wrong with sex before marriage or sex outside of marriage, then what's to stop you? Only morals, values and principles can stop you falling into the trap, and like the man mentioned in Proverbs, going down the path of sexual temptation like an ox to be slaughtered.

My mates say sex is great. How can I argue if I haven't tried it?

Like anything else that's dangerous to experiment with, you don't have to try it to know! Do you want to drink poison to find out whether it kills you or not? Experience is not the only teacher, and what your friends tell you isn't necessarily true. They may be boasting for their own benefit. Then again, they may have found pleasure, but how long will it last? The best sex is experienced in marriage, when you can experiment and enjoy, knowing you are both completely safe and absorbed in an atmosphere of trust.

Don't believe everything you're told, however exciting it seems. It can lead you into situations that can bring lasting regrets.

6

Dealing with relationships

Once you were alienated from God and were enemies in your minds because of your evil behaviour. But now he has reconciled you . . . . Colossians 1:21, 22, NIV.

Many guys have expressed concern about how to develop a good relationship with a girl. In many ways — and as a very general statement — girls seem to have more intuitive skills when it comes to relating. The male is more often accused of being insensitive and uncaring, of failing to notice and of being self-absorbed.

While we don't wish to endorse totally such a blanket generalization, we can understand the concerns. Men behaving badly can give a believable impression that only the physical side of a relationship is important to them. In a recent football tournament one newspaper reported that two supporters had thrown their girl-friends out so that they could concentrate on watching the games! Such extreme actions make the myth of the unromantic male that much more believable.

If there's one non-sexual complaint that we hear more often than any other from girls about their boy-friends it's that they are not romantic. In other words, girls are expecting a certain kind of behaviour, and are disappointed when it doesn't happen. Of course some boys can go 'over the top' and shower their beloved with flowers, gifts, chocolates and the rest. That's not what girls are asking for either.

SO WHAT DO GIRLS REALLY WANT?

Sometimes it really is confusing, isn't it? You get jumbled signals, and mixed reactions.

We remember one boy coming to us, totally puzzled: 'I went to see my girl-friend and when I got there she complained that I never brought her flowers. So next time I took some flowers and she complained that I was just trying to make up for the last time!'

Another perplexed suitor complained that his girl-friend had told him that sex was all boys ever thought about. Not long after she was complaining that he wasn't touching her enough.

For the male mind some of these reactions can be strange. Behind them there is the truth that what girls really want is to be appreciated for what they are as whole and complete people.

As we have mentioned already, and will discuss further in a later chapter, intimacy has been broken down into its sexual parts in the thinking of the modern world. If a girl is just a collection of sexual objects then she will recognize that she is not being appreciated for who she really is.

A couple of comments from the girl's side:

'I keep on catching him looking at my curves!'

Is a girl really impressed when showered with romantic gifts of chocolates, lush flowers and expensive presents?

'He keeps on saying how beautiful I am but I want him to like me because of my personality too.'

In building a relationship you must go beyond the physical appearance. None of us is just what we look like on the outside. Your physical desires may make the visual attractiveness of a girl the most important factor in your mind. But remember that you are not trying to love a doll or a statue but a complex human being. Physical beauty is only one aspect. What about personality, a sense of humour, intelligence, skills, abilities, education, spiritual commitment, honesty, morals and all the rest that make us what we are?

ENDING THE CONFUSION

Take the boy who was confused when told all he thought about was sex and then told off for not touching. What the girl is trying to say is that she wants affection to be expressed in more than just a sexual way. Love and admiration can be shown in light caresses of the hands and face just as much as touching areas normally considered to be 'sexual'.

And the boy-friend who can't get it right whether he brings flowers or not may be showing an attitude that is not appreciated by his girl-friend. You can't expect to come along with a bouquet of flowers and think that this gift makes everything all right. You are not trying to buy love or affection either, or to 'atone' for some wrong by bribery!

You need to be more sensitive to feelings and perceptions. A truly deep relationship is based on mutual understanding. That takes time, and if all you're concerned about is trying to satisfy your physical senses, then you will not be caring much about what she is thinking and experiencing.

Here, then, is another important reason to slow down and talk. Long sessions of physical intimacy without talking do not give an opportunity for a deeper and more meaningful relationship.

SO WHAT SHOULD I DO?

Some boys feel it's important for them to 'make the running' and that the girl expects them to 'try it on'. Not necessarily true. And if you are over-concerned about how you are being judged, then the focus is back on you instead of the two that it takes for a good relationship.

As one guy put it to us, 'I wanted to make sure she thought I was a great lover.' The truth is that truly great lovers are in no rush to satisfy themselves, but have the other person as their highest concern. Remember these words (from 1 Corinthians 13, NEB):

☐ 'Love is patient' — love never feels it has to rush. Rushing indicates something other than love, especially in the early days of a relationship.

☐ 'Love is kind' — love is not hard and hurtful, trying to exploit the other's kindness. Is it really true that girls should be kind, and boys should be cruel? How sad that mistaken rhyme we have heard from boys about girls: 'Treat them mean, keep them keen.' To 'enjoy' being treated mean, and to treat someone you claim to love in a mean way — these are not Christian ways of behaving.

☐ 'Love envies no one' — selfish jealousy is not part of Christian love. What does it say about you if you're concerned that someone else's girl looks better than yours? Love is about finding complete satisfaction in each other — and in this physical looks should not be playing the most important part.

☐ 'Love is never boastful, nor conceited, nor rude' — boasting of yourself, or of what your girl-friend may do for you and so on. This is critical. Never ever share intimate secrets that belong to you and the one you love. How offensive it is to hear of men bragging about their sexual conquests. How repugnant to hear of conceited 'kiss and tell' tales. If you are in love, do not boast but be thankful and make sure your love is reflective of the God of love.

☐ 'Love is not selfish' — if there's anything we would want to underline it's this statement. So many problems in relationships would be immediately resolved if each stopped being selfish. As self-centred, imperfect beings we think of ourselves first, especially in relationships. We can easily look at others and only choose what is good for us. In relationships we are very vulnerable, and so we try to think of Number One and protect our fragile selves. If love was really about thinking of the other first how wonderful and Christlike that love would be!

☐ 'Love is not quick to take offence' — Really? Some 'lovers' seem all too quick to take offence! One word out of place and they're offended all evening. One wrong act and they feel insulted. One smile at the wrong time and they believe they're being laughed at. Those in love are not over-sensitive, and not primarily concerned with themselves and their own prestige.

These words of advice apply equally to both male and female partners! But back to the question of how to relate — truly romantically.

TRUE ROMANCE

True romance, as we've said, is not about giving things; although love is about giving gifts too (which is why sex as the ultimate gift needs to wait until it can truly be completely and utterly given). Romance is about appreciating the one loved for all he or she is — not just the physical part. For that to happen you need to spend time in talking, and not just 'sweet nothings'! If you really are going to spend a lifetime together, you need to know each other extremely well.

A lover's tiff can be painful, raises all the wrong feelings and is often caused by misunderstandings or selfishness.

Use your time together wisely, and not just in seeing 'how far you can go'. Say what you appreciate about the other person, and not just their clothes or body. You need to deepen the relationship, to establish understanding and communication on a meaningful level. So talk about your hopes and dreams, your innermost beliefs. You can't do this and not talk about God, if He is really special for you. To find a spiritual friend with whom you can share without fear of ridicule or contempt is one of the greatest blessings of romance.

Talk about every subject under the sun. Find out how each other's mind works. Work and play together, spend time together with other friends and see how your special friend reacts. See how they relate to their family too. You're not checking as in a test, but you are watching in order to know and understand.

And if things should go wrong for a while, or there is some misunderstanding, then a deep and true romance can come through, stronger and with greater understanding in the end.

REBUILDING RELATIONSHIPS

For it's not in the light-headed days of love-sickness but in the times of trouble that love really shows its character. How you work through your differences, solve problems and overcome challenges, demonstrate what you truly mean to each other.

CONCLUSION

The truth is that in our broken relationships we need God more than ever. As we completely trust in Him, and make sure we are operating from His principles, He can remake us into His image. That's not to say that He will fix relationships so that it seems nothing bad ever happened. God does not wipe memories, but He does help us to deal with them. However the other person responds, by trusting God He will heal your damaged emotions so that your heart will be glad, your tongue will rejoice and your whole being will be at peace. Only God, the divine physician, can ease our troubled feelings and only in His presence will we find true and lasting happiness.

Misunderstandings and problems really put pressure on any couple. They either destroy or strengthen depending on the basis of your relationship.

QUESTIONS AND ANSWERS

So how do you begin a relationship?

That's like asking how to breathe! It should come naturally, or at least without some kind of 'chat-up line'. If you know a girl, then you simply deepen that relationship. If you don't know her, then don't go rushing off thinking you're already in love! You need to get to know her first — that's essential. In the same way as you get into conversation with other people, just start talking. And don't start imagining things beforehand — keep a lid on your imagination and keep it straight. How? Like doing homework together — something normal and natural. And see how it goes from there.

My girl-friend keeps on misunderstanding me. What should I do?

A hard one to answer specifically. It may be she's trying to tell you she's not really interested. Then again it could be a case of mutual misunderstanding in which you are both communicating but not getting the right message! If this is the case, you need to take time out from your normal activities together and sit down and really try and discuss how you are relating to each other. Understanding each other is vital for a developing relationship.

I'm told I'm not naturally romantic. How can I cure this?

There's no medical cure! But you can try and develop your sensitivity to others, and especially to your girl-friend. Try to put your own feelings at the bottom of the list of priorities and see things her way. Don't forget the little things — being polite, considerate, giving small but meaningful gifts and so on. Of course, you may be romantic but have not met the right girl yet!

Just casual, friendly contacts over a game or a meal help you both to get to know one another without heavy emotional pressure.

7

Sexuality – God's gift

So God created human beings, making them to be like himself. He created them male and female. Genesis 1:27.

GOD AND SEX?

That God should be involved in our sexuality is a hard idea for some people. In their eyes God is above all that. As if sex is something sordid and low that has nothing holy and special in it at all.

A terrible mistake to make! For as with everything God ever made, He saw that it was good, even very good. So to make sex into something bad is to fall into the trap of God's Accuser and to believe his lies. For if we can be convinced that sex is evil, then it might as well be treated with contempt. And for those who know differently, that is an awful tragedy.

The truth is that God made us able to experience the heights of sexual pleasure. In this He wanted us to reflect His wonderful love, for as human beings 'make love' in the truest sense of the word then we become like Him. Love that doesn't think of itself, that seeks the best for the other person, that wants to give without limit and not to take.

But sadly many Christians down through the ages have not understood God's gracious gift of sex. Even the great Martin Luther was puzzled by God's creation of humanity as sexual beings and reproduction through sexual intercourse. He commented, 'The reproduction of mankind is a great marvel and mystery. Had God consulted me in the matter, I should have advised Him to continue the generation of the species by fashioning them of clay.'

It surely would have been less risky to go on making human beings out of the dust of the ground! But for us it would have been far less pleasurable and the fact that God *did* indeed give us the gift of sex says something about the kind of God we worship. Though we have often abused His gift this should not blind us to its wonderful potential for the expression of love, remembering that indeed God is love.

So where did all the negative ideas come from? How come the Church so often seems to have a down on sex?

Remember that back in the beginning God said that what He made was *good* — and this applied to man, woman, and sexuality. This theme continued through the Old Testament times, which stressed God's involvement in the natural world. This included God's interest in human sexuality. Sex was seen to be part of the wholeness of the human person, and not a negative part of some split personality.

But Greek ideas came in, and the body came to be seen as evil, and the spirit or soul as good. This meant that sex was associated with sin, since all things physical were viewed as part of an evil world. The goal was to allow the spirit to develop, and eventually to leave the 'prison house' of the body at death.

This new kind of 'theology' or understanding of humanity invaded the early Church. So people tried to leave physical temptations behind them, and went into monasteries and convents.

This led to a number of errors.

The Fall. The story of human sin became linked with sexuality, some Christians even believing that sex was a *result* of sin. The idea of sex-

MISTAKEN IDEAS ABOUT GOD AND SEX

Take a look at some common ideas that involve God and sex. Then see how many are NOT true!

T	F	
☐	☐	God will stop your girl-friend getting pregnant if you're really sorry for going too far.
☐	☐	God made us the way we are so what happens is His responsibility.
☐	☐	Because sex is physical then God isn't interested in the subject.
☐	☐	If you pray to God hard enough He will take away all your sexual desires.
☐	☐	God has made it so Christians have the best sex.
☐	☐	God has made it so Christians have the worst sex.
☐	☐	God made us to be guilty about sex.
☐	☐	Because God hasn't said anything about masturbation, oral sex and so on it must mean that whatever He hasn't banned is OK.
☐	☐	When God forgives your sexual sin, it makes everything right.
☐	☐	God says sex is only for having children.

None of these statements is true! Some are obviously false, others may cause some discussion. For example, while God may forgive you, this doesn't wipe out all the consequences of your sin. Healing of sin comes, but the memory is not wiped. And when someone else is involved, then it is much more complicated again.

ual corruption through the Fall, or of sex being God's punishment, hardly makes for a positive view of sexuality. The shame of Adam and Eve realizing they were naked after eating the forbidden fruit led to the idea that sex was an evil that came from sin. And so sex was seen as a sin to be avoided if you could.

Rise of celibacy. The fact that Jesus never married was taken as the great ideal for His followers. Other examples like John the Baptist and Paul were quoted as the best way for a Christian to live, and some of Paul's writings were used to prove this position. Being unmarried was even adopted as the preferred state for the priesthood as it developed through the centuries. The highest state of Christianity was to live as a monk or nun far from any temptation, sexual or otherwise.

The virgin birth. This was taken to mean that God frowned on sex, since Jesus was conceived without sexual union. The idea of Mary having any kind of sexual desire was to be rejected, and even her own conception eventually declared 'immaculate' — that is, not the product of sexual intercourse. This was linked to ideas of 'original sin' and Mary had to be seen as pure and without sin, so even her birth was believed not to be the result of intercourse either.

Reaction to paganism. The world in which Christians lived was often very perverse and permissive when it came to sexual matters. In order to

RIGHT SEX

Sex in God's eyes is a physical sign of oneness. It shows how closely you are joined — you are united, together, one. That's why sex outside of marriage can be so destructive — because it can turn something that joins you together into something that forces you apart. Even within marriage, sex is not always so pleasurable at the start. Sex may be uncomfortable, even painful for the woman. And the man may be too eager, and may not take the time to satisfy his wife.

Sex in marriage is a time for learning together so that it does become right for both. This can hardly happen when sex is a casual affair, without the loving support and care that marriage brings. Sexual failure outside of marriage is more painful because you do not have that support to carry you through, and so it can cause great damage. Sex is powerful, yet so fragile, that it needs to be part of a stable and trusting atmosphere to grow and develop.

Only then can sex be totally RIGHT!

remain separate from such practices, the Church tended to be very defensive. Origen, one early Church father, took such ideas to an extreme, and castrated himself to prove to himself that sex could no longer tempt him.

THE INFLUENCE OF CHURCH LEADERS

Augustine was a very respected church leader. He had not always been a Christian, and had indulged in sexual affairs. Much of his struggles appear to have a sexual component. His cry of 'Make me pure — but not yet' reflects his fight with sexual desire and, in dealing with this, it seems that he decided in the end that the only way was to deny sexuality altogether. His influence on the doctrine and practice of the Church was very great. It is sad that such a great man was not better able to deal with what was for him a great temptation, and that his personal struggles became the teachings of the Church.

His ideas developed the thought that sexual desire was the way in which original sin was passed on through the generations, along with the belief that the Fall had brought about uncontrollable sexual lust in man. Obviously such concepts have more to do with Augustine than the Bible.

For Augustine the best state was celibacy — not to marry. However he went further, seeing marriage as some kind of relief for sinful desires. So he permitted marriage for those

Wholesome sexual enjoyment within a permanent relationship was denied by some Church fathers as inherently sinful.

who 'burned'. However, even within marriage sex was only for procreation.

These ideas became a whole system which the Church taught for many generations. They still affect some people today.

A system of thought that taught the basic sinfulness of sex obviously influenced many people for the worse. To be told by the Church, for example at the Council of Trent in the sixteenth century, that they should abstain from sex during Lent to become more spiritual, made the

Church's ideas about the depraving and corrupting effects of sex very clear.

What did all this mean to the way in which women were viewed? The answer is that women were a great contradiction!

If the woman was spiritual but not sexual, she was elevated to the position of great honour. Many of those counted as saints were women, and highly respected. On the other hand, a woman could be sexual, but absolutely not spiritual. She could be seen (and even accepted) as a sexual being, though dangerous.

In no way could the two be joined in the same woman. A spiritual *and* sexual woman was, for the Church, a contradiction in terms.

Tertullian, an early Church writer, said that women were 'the devil's gateway'. Monks were not allowed even to talk to a woman alone on pain of flogging with two hundred lashes. One abbott was punished for allowing a woman to be buried in abbey grounds. Even her dead body desecrated holiness!

By the end of the fourth century priests were forbidden to marry. The sexes were separated so that they could live celibate lives in monasteries and nunneries. And this system has operated for many hundreds of years.

While Luther rightly rejected some of the prevailing ideas in the Church, and married a former nun, he still held generally to Augustine's view of sex as some kind of 'necessary evil' for the production of children. Calvin, too, married, but admitted that celibacy was still an ideal and made a list of what he considered to be sexual sin (both within and outside of marriage).

JUST FOR HAVING KIDS?

Linked to such negative ideas about physical sex has been the idea that it was only intended to keep the human race going: sex is for procreation only. Once again this idea did not originate in the church, but gradually seeped in.

A couple of examples, this time from Latin writers:

'Sexual desire has been given to man not for the gratification of pleasure but for the continuance of the human race.' *Seneca*.

'We should not have sexual connection for the sake of pleasure, but only for the sake of begetting good children.' *Lucanus*.

Put together these ideas and, pretty soon, sex ends up just as a necessary evil, something that has to be done as a duty in order to have children. And the natural result of this was celibacy — avoiding sex altogether — the concept that to be really holy you gave up any thought of sex. Eventually this idea is what led to the monasteries and convents. Whatever happened to God's plan for sexual joy in a happy relationship? For centuries it was consigned to brothels, rarely spoken of and generally despised. Another tragedy of mistaken ideas of God and His purposes.

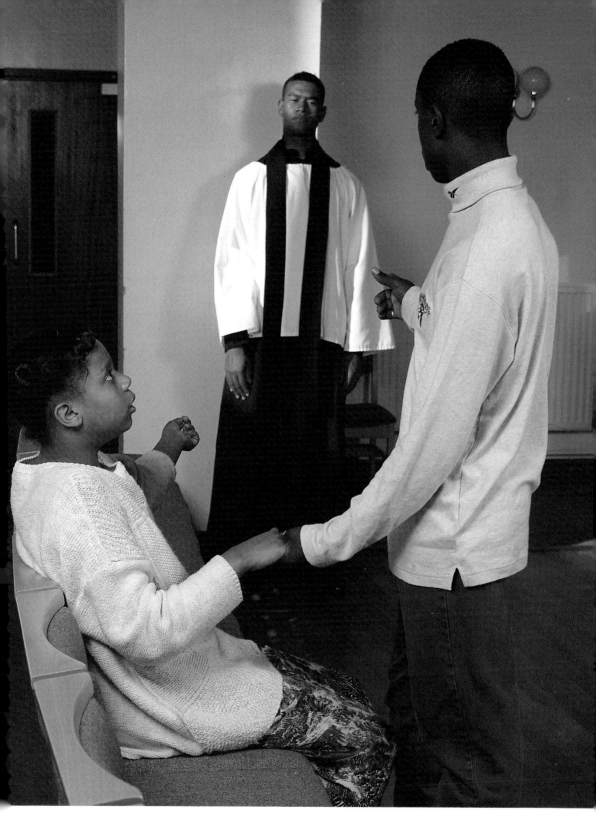

It is a sad fact that the Church has long been looked upon as the spoiler of anything enjoyable. Its anti-sex stand has more to do with misguided tradition than Biblical teaching.

CHURCH AND SEX TODAY

A negative attitude towards sexuality still exists today in the Church. It is not only a non-biblical view of sexuality, it is anti-biblical, because it goes against what God has said. Sex is not to be seen as reflecting the animal in us, or of only being tolerated to produce children.

We need to have the freedom to discuss frankly and honestly the rights and wrongs of sexual principles and behaviour so that church members can make good decisions. One of the current dangers is that because the Church's old views about sex are now seen to be wrong and out-dated, people throw away all restraint and say that any kind of sex is acceptable. But the moral beliefs still apply today, and for ever. So we must be careful to keep the good, and throw out the bad views the Church has had about sex.

Just because everybody else is liberal and permissive, does not mean Christians have to follow suit. Our foundation is God Himself, and He has already told us the right way to use His miraculous gift of creative sexuality.

Sex is truly creative — in the exploring of each other and in the possibility of creating a new life. In this way we reflect the creative power of God, whether a child is conceived or not. This is the *making* of love.

And so we must stay true to the Bible, which is very clear in its presentation of sex — how it can be right, and how it can be wrong. The

What I think the Church believes about sex

Y	N	
☐	☐	Sex is dirty.
☐	☐	Sex is only for marriage.
☐	☐	You're not supposed to enjoy having sex.
☐	☐	Sex is just for having babies.
☐	☐	Before marriage you can do anything else sexual except intercourse.
☐	☐	Sexual sins are worse than other sins.
☐	☐	Sex is not meant to be talked about.
☐	☐	Sex is a gift from God.
☐	☐	You will be punished by God for messing around with sex.
☐	☐	What you do with sex is up to you.

An enjoyable sex life within a secure, close, loving relationship is God's way to provide for loved and balanced children. Much of the increase in juvenile crime can be traced to insecure, broken homes as a result of permissive sex.

power of our sexuality can't be denied. It's how we use it that affects us.

But, remembering that God said He made everything (including our sexuality) 'very good', let's look first at the misuse of sex.

THE BIBLE AND IMMORAL SEX

The misuse of sex is another aspect of sin. We must be very clear about this. In many of today's societies, the biblical ideas of sexual sin have been abandoned. It's OK to have affairs. It's OK to commit adultery. It's OK to have sex before marriage and so on.

But if we take the Bible as the Word of God, then sin must be called by its right name. We cannot say that the misuse of sex is OK, or that no harm comes from it. To say that wrong is right, that sin is not sin, helps no one.

Only by accepting our sinfulness

can we be helped. Only by seeing our terrible misuse of God's gift of sex can the damage be repaired. Only by agreeing that our evil desires are wrong can we become healed, happy, and whole in our sexuality.

So let's agree with God when He says to us in the Bible:

'What human nature does is quite plain. It shows itself in immoral, filthy, and indecent actions; in worship of idols and witchcraft. People become enemies and they fight; they become jealous, angry, and ambitious. They separate into parties and groups; they are envious, get drunk, have orgies, and do other things like these. I warn you now as I have before: those who do these things will not possess the Kingdom of God.' Galatians 5:19-21.

Notice, though, that this does not just talk about sexual sins. Rather, sexual sins are just part of an 'anti-God' character that involves many other sins. It's not surprising, then, that the acceptance of sexual sins is part of a world that has just about rejected God. Our very human nature without God has sexual misconduct as a component part.

So what do we do, as Christians? What happens to us as we choose God and His converting power?

'For when we lived according to our human nature, the sinful desires stirred up by the Law were at work in our bodies, and all we did ended in death. Now, however, we are free from the Law, because we died to

The misuse of sex is part of the degenerating moral scene that has accompanied the rejection of Christianity.

that which once held us prisoners. No longer do we serve in the old way of a written law, but in the new way of the Spirit.' Romans 7:5, 6.

The Law of sin and death is the rule by which we used to live, dominated by our sinful nature. Evil is a powerful controlling force that directs us to wrong. Our desires to sin come from this 'Law'. But now, with Jesus, we are made free from this 'compulsion' towards evil. We don't *have* to follow our darker side that looks for selfish pleasure at the cost of others. Now we are free to follow the good of the Spirit, which leads us to all that is pure and righteous:

'But the Spirit produces love, joy, peace, patience, kindness, goodness, faithfulness, humility, and self-control. There is no law against such things as these. And those who belong to Christ Jesus have put to death their human nature with all its passions and desires.' Galatians 5:22-24.

Of course, this process doesn't happen overnight. And remember, you're not looking to get rid of a healthy sexual attitude, just the wrong aspects of sex:

'You must work to put to death, then, the earthly desires at work in you, such as sexual immorality, indecency, lust, evil passions, and greed (for greed is a form of idolatry).' Colossians 3:5.

And this we don't do by ourselves. It's part of the grace of God that He gives us, showing us that our perverted view of sex is really not going to be good for us, and wanting to give us so much better sexual ideas and experiences:

'For God has revealed his grace for the salvation of the whole human race. That grace instructs us to give up ungodly living and worldly passions, and to live self-controlled, upright, and godly lives in this world.' Titus 2:11, 12.

'Avoid immorality. Any other sin a man commits does not affect his body; but the man who is guilty of sexual immorality sins against his own body. Don't you know that your body is the temple of the Holy Spirit, who lives in you and who

was given to you by God? You do not belong to yourselves but to God; he bought you for a price. So use your bodies for God's glory.' 1 Corinthians 6:18-20.

When we're told to use our bodies for God's glory, that also means sexually! That is the context of the verse — and so we praise and glorify God in the right use of our sexuality.

As a result, notice how we all are to live as Christians:

Those who see the Bible as being anti-sex, hard and empty of pleasure have gone for the ideas the Church once mistakenly promoted and have missed its real issues.

'Since you are God's people, it is not right that any matters of sexual immorality or indecency or greed should even be mentioned among you. Nor is it fitting for you to use language which is obscene, profane, or vulgar. Rather you should give thanks to God. You may be sure that no one who is immoral, indecent, or greedy (for greed is a form of idolatry) will ever receive a share in the Kingdom of Christ and of God.' Ephesians 5:3-5.

What does God want for you, sexually? He wants the best! And that can only be by following the best way, which is God's way, our Creator and Redeemer: 'God wants you to be holy and completely free from sexual immorality.' (1 Thessalonians 4:3.) So why not make a solemn promise to live as God has advised, and make a promise like Job: 'I have made a solemn promise never to look with lust at a girl.' (Job 31:1.)

THE BIBLE'S SONG OF SEXUAL LOVE

Having read all the above, don't conclude that God is against sex itself. Rather, sex *in the wrong context* is what is being condemned. We've saved the best till last. For the Bible speaks wonderfully about sex in the right situation. Just read these selections from the Song of Solomon:

'Your lips cover me with kisses; your love is better than wine. There is a fragrance about you; the sound of your name recalls it. No woman could help loving you. Take me with you, and we'll run away . . . .' *The Woman*. (1:2-4.)

'How beautiful you are, my love; how your eyes shine with love!' *The Man*. (1:15.)

'I am weak from passion. His left hand is under my head, and his right hand caresses me.' *The Woman*. (2:5, 6.)

'Come then, my love; my darling, come with me.' *The Man*. (2:10.)

'My lover is mine, and I am his.' *The Woman*. (2:16.)

'How beautiful you are, my love! How your eyes shine with love . . . your hair dances . . . your teeth are white . . . your lips are like a scarlet ribbon . . . your cheeks glow . . . your neck is like the tower of David, round and smooth . . . your breasts are like gazelles . . . how perfect you are!' *The Man*. (4:1-7.)

'Close your heart to every love but mine; hold no one in your arms but me. Love is as powerful as death; passion is as strong as death itself. It bursts into flame and burns like a raging fire . . .

'I am a wall, and my breasts are its towers. My lover knows that with him I find contentment and peace.' *The Woman*. (8:6, 10.)

Remember this is Scripture! What do you do with this? Are you embarrassed by it, or ashamed of its frank language? Or can you see God's hand in inspiring these words which speak of the rightness of sexuality?

What wonderful poetry that celebrates human love, of the desire and longing of a man and a woman in love! And to make this a part of the Holy Scriptures says some wonderful things about God too! Though the Church has in the past had difficulty accepting the description of the intensity of human love, and has tried to make it a spiritual description of Christ's love for the Church, it is without doubt firstly a wonderful song in tribute to God's gift of sexual love.

And remember, God's wish is that each of His children find true happiness, and if this is through sexual expression, then in the wonderful love between husband and wife: 'May your fountain be blessed, and may you rejoice in the wife of your youth. A loving doe, a graceful deer — may her breasts satisfy you always, may you ever be captivated by her love.' Proverbs 5:18, 19, NIV.

So let us accept the gift, so freely given, and use it wisely and well to God's glory.

God has designed us to be attracted to and to love that special person, to be loved for whom we are, to enjoy sexual expression only within a permanent commitment to one another. That is the gift God has given us — and it's great!

QUESTIONS AND ANSWERS

Why did God make something right so wrong?

Well that depends on how you view sex. The excuse, 'It felt so right', can mean that you were just carried away with your own physical pleasure. And if that's what sex is reduced to, then it can be very wrong. But as we've tried to explain, God intended sex to be wonderfully right — the way that you could show the height and depth of your love to another human being. Sex is only wrong when it's misused. Like fire, which can heat your home or cook your food. That's good. But it can also burn down your home if it is misused. And that can be extremely bad. So sex is right and wrong, depending on how you and your partner use the precious gift that has been so lovingly placed in your hands by a caring God.

Why do I feel so guilty about sex when I'm in church?

We don't know exactly why, but we're sure it must be to do with the way you view sex, and also perhaps with what you've done. For if you know that the Church teaches certain sexual behaviour is wrong, and you've done just that, then no wonder you feel guilty. And you need to sort that out, in your own life, and find God's forgiveness.

But it could be possible to feel guilty even if you haven't done anything wrong. You may believe your thoughts are sinful. Or you may even think that any kind of mention of sex is wrong and gives you guilt feelings. This can be in part due to your upbringing, or what certain Church leaders have said. But as we've stated, sex of itself is not to be seen as evil. Only wrongly using sex. As Paul says, it's the *love* of money that's evil, not money itself. And it's the misuse of sex that is evil, not sex itself.

If God sees everything, won't He see me having sex? That idea really puts me off.

Yes, God does see everything. But He's not a super snooper! He surely respects our privacy, and allows us our own freedom of choice. Of course, if you are doing something you believe He has forbidden, then it's not surprising it will put you off. But in a good and right marriage relationship, look again at the Song of Solomon and thank the God who made us to have pleasure and enjoyment.

I don't think we should talk about sex at church. After all, it's a private matter.

Such thinking has often been at the root of problems for Christians. Why? Because if we do not speak about sexuality in a Christian context, then we allow other views about sex to direct our thoughts. Yes, sexual activity is a private matter between husband and wife, but the principles are given very clearly in the Bible and we need to understand them. Like any other sin, the misuse of sex must be clearly explained so that Christians can know good from evil. To simply tell a newly-married couple to 'follow their instincts' will not necessarily lead to a happy marriage. And when many in the church have already crashed off the sexual rails we need to make sure the biblical view of sexuality is very clearly explained in the right church setting.

I find it hard to think about sex and God at the same time. Is that wrong?

It's not unusual is perhaps the quickest answer. And that is because most people have not taken the time to think about God as the Creator of our sexuality, the One who has given us such a wonderful gift. If you understand that, and wish to use sex wisely and well, then you should not have this problem. Difficulties often occur when people have already experimented with sex in the wrong way, and then realize that they are going against God. If this is true for you, you need to change your sex life and make sure it is in harmony with what God says.

How are Christians to deal with sex in a sex-mad world?

The Christian reaction must be balanced. To close our minds to what is happening in the world is practically impossible, and simply to shut it all out may mean for some denying sexuality altogether. Nor, very obviously, should we run headfirst into this sex-mad world, as you call it. Christians need to see again the God-focused nature of sex,

Happiness for a newly married couple doesn't come from just following their instincts. A biblical view of sexuality needs to be understood to avoid problems.

and praise and thank Him for it. It's not something we dreamed up; sex is not a human invention. It came from God, and it is for our good. The Devil has taken sex and perverted and debased it, but we do not need to follow such ideas. Rather, we need to promote God's gift of sexuality as part of His plan for humanity, as a wonderful expression of true love between a man and a woman, not just some slaking of lust or self-satisfaction.

Living with the constant fear that God has your behaviour under constant scrutiny is often due to the mistaken idea that God looks upon sex as sinful.

What about the church's attitude to sins and sexual sins? Are they any different?

It sometimes seems that way, doesn't it? Perhaps sexual sins are more visible; or is it that they seem to threaten people more? Whatever the case, sexual sins have frequently been viewed in the church as particularly bad. However, we must keep a proper perspective here, whatever our own personal reaction to sexual sins. Does God see them as being particularly different from other vices? Sin is sin, some say — and there's truth in that. On the other hand, the impact of sexual sin on relationships can be so severe that they do have a major practical impact, and the church does well to treat such very seriously. Of one thing we're sure — there is no sin that God cannot forgive — except for the sin you don't want forgiven.

Should the church be involved in speaking about sex?

Yes, absolutely. In the past, the church may not have expressed itself very well, but that's no reason to give up. Besides, if the church doesn't speak, there are many others who will, and their ideas about sex may be a long way from what the Bible teaches. While Christians are right to emphasize the intimate nature of sex, to remain silent is very dangerous and foolish, especially when the world's view is so very different.

8

Weary of the theory?

Avoid the passions of youth, and strive for righteousness, faith, love, and peace, together with those who with a pure heart call out to the Lord for help. 2 Timothy 2:22.

Sex in theory is one thing. It's very different trying to put the theory into practice. And as one young man told us once, it's easy to get 'weary of the theory'! For:

☐ You may agree that it is good to keep sex until you're married.

☐ You may decide that you've gone too far with your girl-friend and wish to stop.

☐ You may reject pornography as wrong.

But when it comes to reality, situations can be difficult. You may have the principles, but the practice is another question. Most Christians recognize that they have not lived up to their ideals, especially in the area of their sexual behaviour. But that's no reason to ditch the principles. You just need to work through what the theory really does mean when you come to sexual situations.

☐ Take the first example. You're going to wait. You have a girl-friend, and you're already 'getting involved'.

What if she makes it clear that she wants to sleep with you? You may even have discussed marriage, or are engaged. Is the sexual invitation so easy to resist? You know the theory, but 'instant pleasure' is being offered you. What do you choose in this situation?

You may even think you have to. Otherwise you believe you will be less than a man or something. Only if you have a very clear idea of the very real practical dangers and potential disasters of premarital sex will you be able to say 'No'. (And this means more than physical dangers; the spiritual and mental dangers are perhaps even more important, along with the potential to totally destroy the love-relationship.)

☐ What about the second situation — wanting to stop some sexual behaviour you've already begun? Again theory can be hard to put into practice. After all, you've 'already sinned'. So why stop now?

You can't go back, can you? What's done is done.

See how you can convince yourself to continue, even when you know you're wrong? And when you're in the same situation for that sexual activity to occur, it becomes so hard to say 'No'. What will she think of me? Maybe she already thinks badly of me for doing this. Or maybe she will think me foolish for saying no now, after what we've done already. See how complicated it gets?

The important fact is that you will never develop a good relationship if you believe you're not behaving properly. You both need to be comfortable with what is happening, and if you are not, then there is not much chance of a good and happy future relationship. That's why sexual principles are so important — they keep you right until the time is right!

☐ Then what of situation three? Yes, you have identified pornography as wrong. But a friend of yours gives you a magazine to look at. Maybe it's not too bad — not hardcore porn. But there are pictures of girls in revealing poses. Do you throw the magazine away? Or do you politely refuse? Or does your curiosity get the better of you and you want to take a look? After all, you convince yourself, I should learn about sex. I need to know what to do. This is just part of my education, right?

Again the principle is com-promised by the practice. And perhaps, before you know it, you're going out and buying such magazines for yourself, just to 'continue your education'.

Only by seeing where such thinking leads, and the sad results of an addiction to pornography, will you want to say no in the first place.

That's why this chapter deals with some very **practical** advice.

FACTOR 1. **Your thoughts.** If, like the people before the Flood, the thoughts of your heart are only evil continually, (see Gen. 6:5), you obviously have a major problem. And letting your thoughts wander and run free, especially in the area of sex, can be very damaging. For as you think in your heart, so you are (Prov. 23:7).

One boy confided that he had a particular sexual problem. How often did he think about it? 'All the time' was his answer. Obviously he had a very unhealthy attitude, and his most important need was to change his thought patterns.

This is even true in some Christian presentations. Confessions and conversion stories can often concentrate on the sins and evils that have been given up, and not on the new life in Jesus. Even preachers can so concentrate on the vice they are condemning that this seems to be more important than the solution! We must not fill our minds with evil, even when trying to speak against it.

FACTOR 2. **Your conversation and behaviour.** Be sure to keep your speech pure, your actions right and true. You may count yourself as a Christian, but your actions must reflect your beliefs. So watch what you are saying and doing, because you can give opportunity for temptation or misunderstanding. Remember that others watch you, especially if you claim high principles, and will be waiting to see how you operate.

FACTOR 3. **Your entertainment, books, films, places you go.** We're always surprised when young people who come for counsel don't realize the influences their choices of entertainment have on them. How can you stay in good spiritual health if your diet has no spiritual food? And how do you keep from falling into temptation when you spend your time in places which are hardly Christian?

FACTOR 4. **Your relationship with God.** You must keep in touch! How can you count God as a Friend if you don't spend time talking together and sharing your concerns?

The pub, bar or club is seen by many teenagers as the social thing — but for Christians is it really the place to encourage spiritual growth?

Sport can be a healthy way to relieve stress and to engage your mind when thoughts you don't want dominate your thinking.

While a few can become fanatical, the greatest problem is forgetting about God and Christian principles when it comes to your intimate relationships.

So how do I change my thoughts, conversation, behaviour, entertainment — especially those that I know are wrong? (Notice that not all sexual thoughts are wrong!)

Distractions. Find other subjects that interest you. Work, hobbies, sports, games, all kinds of other interests that will occupy your mind and give you other kinds of pleasure. For life is more than sex!

Bible reading and prayer. God's support is vital. But be careful not to become over-involved or obsessed by your problem. Sometimes focusing on a problem can make it worse. Just pray for God to work with you in dealing with what concerns you, and then move on. Don't spend all your time thinking about it. This can simply increase the possibility of falling into temptation.

True friends. You need to choose your friends well. Make sure they have wisdom and good judgement, and high principles. You can find enjoyment together in good clean fun, and if you go out together as a group you can meet and become friendly with girls in a good setting.

A confidant to help. Some kind of counsellor — whether formal or informal — can be of great value. Again, this person needs to be mature and responsible, and totally confidential. You need to be able to trust this person, the more so if you are seeking help with personal problems. Your church minister can give you guidance in this area.

KEEPING SEX GOOD

The great modern myth is that sexuality is only to do with the genital organs. The great objective of sexual satisfaction is to achieve orgasm — just about at any cost, it seems. As a result, the relationship between male and female is reduced to this 'lowest common denominator' of satisfying the sexual drive through genital sex.

This sexual 'heresy' has multiple dangers. The obvious hazard is that every participant views others as a kind of sexual commodity and is so viewed in turn. If the end result is

Make friends by being friendly. Go out as part of a group. This way you can find out what people are like without getting involved too deeply.

understood as having to be sexual intercourse, then inevitably this will be what happens — a kind of self-fulfilling prophecy. A sort of sexual fatalism develops: 'We all know what's going to happen, so I might as well go with the flow.'

Alternatively the fear of relationships having to be sexual can lead some to avoid the company of the opposite sex entirely. The feeling that safety is found with the lads can mean problems in any eventual relationship with a girl, since many misunderstandings can develop along with false expectations and anxieties over the physical requirements of sex.

The truth is that when a man and woman relate to one another the difference in their sex will always play some role. That's not to say that such relationships are driven by the need for genital sex. Rather the dif-

CASE STUDIES

These are some case studies we have used in seminars we've conducted. These have proved excellent ways of generating thought and discussion about sexual situations. In giving good advice from a Christian viewpoint, other young people have been helped themselves. So you decide what advice you would give, if asked:

JOHN believes he has a very high sex drive. He finds himself thinking about sex a great deal. He wishes to be true to his high Christian ideals, but often fails. He has read what Jesus said about having lust in his eye, and is worried. He has been trying to give up the practice of masturbation, and is desperately seeking advice. He confides in you as one of his closest friends. What do you tell him?

MARTHA and ROBERT have been going out for more than a year now. At first they found it quite easy to keep to limited contact — kissing and cuddling — but now both find that they want to go further. They don't know what the real limit is as Christians, and are concerned that things may soon get out of hand. They believe that they are truly in love, and plan to get married as soon as they have finished their studies. If you were asked for advice, what would it be?

ALFRED has just come to you with 'a little problem'. He confesses he has been gay ever since he can remember and yet, as a baptized Christian, knows that the Church teaches this is wrong. Some of his homosexual friends from another Church say that their Church teaches that being gay isn't a sin any more. He is confused, and really wants to change. He is trying to find a girl-friend, but admits he's not really attracted to women. He wants

ferent aspects of sexuality as found in men and women colour and enhance the interaction, and bring interest and life to shared experiences and conversations. This is part of God's intention, and reveals His gift of shared differentness which makes life so interesting! Our distinct sexualities are part of who we are, and we cannot and should not deny them since they affect the way we think and react. Human sexuality is to be respected and admired, not seen as some depraved consequence of sin. And remember: the penis is not equipped with a brain so it should not be used for thinking with! Your thinking needs to be done *before* you get into a physical relationship.

HOW FAR IS TOO FAR

Is it just a question of drawing lines? Lines in your thoughts, lines answers to his questions. Do you have any?

REBECCA arrives on your doorstep one evening in a terrible state. She is hysterical, but eventually you discover she has been raped. She is too frightened to say anything more, and doesn't want to do anything about it. Do you agree with her, and how would you counsel her?

JIM is a close friend at church. He is outwardly a happy and attractive person, but one day you happen to see him buying a 'girlie' magazine in a local shop. He doesn't see you, and you say nothing to him. As a Christian is it your duty to confront him with sin, or to say nothing since it is a private matter? How would you help him with his problem if you did raise the subject?

RACHEL has been 'coming on' to Tim very strongly. Tim doesn't want to get caught out, and is trying to resist her. She makes it very clear that she is sexually attracted to him, and hints at 'great pleasures' if he will go out with her. Tim admits to being sexually stimulated by her suggestions, but wants to keep true to his Christian principles. What would you advise him to do?

HANNAH has come to see you. She's been going out with your best friend David for several months. She tells you that they 'nearly went too far' and that David is pleading to give him 'what he needs'. She wants you to go and talk to David about the situation, because she says she can't stand all the pressure he's putting on her to have full sex. Would you agree to her request, and if so what would you say to David, remembering you are best friends?

Now think about how you have tried to give good advice for others, and see how you would advise someone who had a similar problem to your own.

on the human body? No: before you can talk about this, you must agree the basic principles of love, respect and goodness — the spiritual dimension. For what good is any definition of how far to go when you don't really care anyway? Remember that true love is not selfish and demanding, but thinks of the other person and of what will be ultimately best.

But we have already accepted this, right? And it is helpful to speak very practically, instead of just giving theoretical ideas. Remember what we talked about when we discussed the human sexual response. How it's like a graph that curves upwards. The further you go up the line, the more intense the feelings, and the harder to go back!

So when you are with your girlfriend be aware of what you are doing to each other. Just because it may feel good doesn't mean it is necessarily helpful! Nor is your own conscience always the best guide, because you may already have fooled yourself into thinking, 'There's nothing wrong in doing this.' Nor is it OK to tell yourselves: 'As long as we don't have sexual intercourse, everything else is OK.'

Making love begins with the first touch. The progression leads on from there. Through kissing and caressing, to fondling each other and genital stimulation. And if you want our best advice, once you are touching each other's genitals, you are already too far down the road.

Why? Because it's hard to return from this point, though of course not impossible. Also you need to be aware that some girls are extremely stimulated by having their breasts touched, so do not take advantage of this.

Because in the end it is both of you who are to blame if you lose control. Don't ever forget that sex is a question of choice. You cannot say 'I got carried away' because even in that you made decisions. You made a decision to spend time alone. You put yourself in a certain situation. You maybe spent long hours in kissing sessions. You excited each other to fever pitch. Or, worse still, you even forced your way against the girl's will, and what now? All this can come from rejecting the need to make decisions *beforehand*. And not avoiding situations which might lead to problems, or spending too long in intimate time alone. As Jeremiah noted, 'The heart is deceitful above all things, who can know it.' In that sense, however good your intentions are, don't trust yourself! Don't rush to get too physical, and take the time for developing not just a physical but an emotional and spiritual relationship too. Keep God involved!

DEALING WITH TEMPTATION

☐ First of all, be honest with yourself — and God. Don't fool your conscience into thinking it's all right when it's all wrong. For example, what are you doing when you say that as long as we're not having 'full

HOW FAR SHOULD YOU GO?

Remember this is a question of drawing lines — not on bodies, but in your head. We're talking about principles here, not bans. So tick whether you agree or disagree with the statement:

	AGREE	DISAGREE
It doesn't matter how far you go.	☐	☐
If you're in love, you can do what you want.	☐	☐
If you start touching each other below the waist you're in real trouble.	☐	☐
Christians shouldn't do any more than kissing.	☐	☐
God is involved in all areas of my life, including me and my girl-friend.	☐	☐
If you're a real Christian, you don't need to worry. God will take care of any situation.	☐	☐
Long hours spent kissing and cuddling alone can be dangerous because you can take things further.	☐	☐
Once you've done something you shouldn't, there's no point in trying to stop.	☐	☐
You need to decide what is acceptable before you get involved.	☐	☐
Oral sex is better than doing the real thing, so that's OK.	☐	☐

sex' then you're following God's commands? Isn't oral sex or mutual masturbation very similar to sex? If so, does that make this substitute acceptable? If it is sin then make sure you call it sin. You need to think seriously about what sexual immorality really does mean in practice.

☐ Then you also must avoid temptation. It's not enough to say 'I won't', and then put yourself into a situation where it is likely that you will. As one couple told us, they often used to fool around until one day they 'found' themselves naked on a bed and just about to have sexual intercourse. Then they realized what they were about to do. They did stop, but they admitted it was *extremely* difficult. Our question was why they were naked on a bed together anyway? Remember the car illustration? It would be like speeding straight towards a brick wall and leaving it to the last minute to hit the brakes. Is that any way to drive? Is that any way to treat a car either? So think about yourselves, and your bodies.

☐ Thirdly, understand how temptation works. The Bible describes the process very clearly:

'A person is tempted when he is drawn away and trapped by his own evil desire. Then his evil desire conceives and gives birth to sin; and sin, when it is full-grown, gives birth to death.' (see James 1:14, 15.)

You have a thought. You dwell on this tempting thought and link it to your own sinful desire. This grows and fills your mind until you decide to act on your desire, and actually commit this sin, which in turn leads to spiritual death. If you understand this process, then you can do something about making sure you don't keep those tempting thoughts running round inside your head. And don't think you can do it, because you're stronger/better/holier than others. You can't. Like a fire, sin will undoubtedly burn you and hurt you:

'Can you carry fire against your chest without burning your clothes? Can you walk on hot coals without burning your feet? It is just as dangerous to sleep with another man's wife. Whoever does it will suffer.' Proverbs 6:27-29.

Not because God comes in with vengeance to punish such sinners, but because the very sin brings its own terrible results. Adultery, fornication, infidelity, promiscuity, immorality — whatever you call it, has the same disastrous consequences.

So, as Solomon advises again, 'When sinners tempt you, my son, don't give in.' Proverbs 1:10. Anyone who wants to tempt you and lead you astray is not thinking of your good, or is a true friend. For, 'Sin must no longer rule in your mortal bodies, so that you obey the desires of your natural self. Nor must you surrender any part of yourselves to sin to be used for wicked purposes.' Romans 6:12, 13.

Realize the kind of person you are. We all have tendencies in us to evil. So admit this, and do not give any scope for these evil desires to have any opportunity. What seems like a 'good time' may really be a total disaster:

'For what our human nature wants is opposed to what the Spirit wants, and what the Spirit wants is opposed to what our human nature wants. These two are enemies, and this means that you cannot do what you want to do.' Galatians 5:17.

So follow this excellent advice, given to a young man: 'Avoid the passions of youth, and strive for righteousness, faith, love, and peace, together with those who with a pure heart call out to the Lord for help.' 2 Timothy 2:22.

To summarize:

☐ Admit your sinfulness and ask

It's important to find out the interests you both can get involved in. It helps to consolidate your friendship and is also a guard against sexual situations that overtake your principles.

God for help.

☐ Don't say wrong is right.

☐ Make sure you don't lead yourself into temptation — avoid sexual situations. You know where you go to sin — so don't go.

☐ Spend time with your girl-friend in things other than intimate physical exploration. Don't have snorkel-ling kissing sessions (when you only come up for air). Realize that too long alone can be dangerous.

☐ Know how temptation works, and don't give the Devil opportunity by dwelling on sexual thoughts.

☐ Most of all, crowd out evil with good. It *is* true that the Devil finds work for idle hands to do.

WHY WAIT?

'If' is the beginning of most of those questions about virginity. 'After all,' says one young man, 'we're going to be married soon. What does a ceremony and a piece of paper matter if we truly love each other?'

The answer is in the question. *If you truly love one another* then there's no reason *not* to wait until marriage for full sexual expression. If you really do love, why make love subject to your sexual demands, however insistent? Why risk all the negative aspects of sex before marriage when you will be able to enjoy each other totally and fully very soon — and in the right situation!

OK. What are these negative results of sex before marriage? We believe you should make up your mind with all the evidence. Just because others are doing it is no reason for you to follow. Nor is it enough just to be told, 'Don't do it!' You need to know for yourself why.

☐ *Mental reasons.* First off, sex

MY REASONS TO WAIT

Tick those reasons you think are important to you as reasons to wait until marriage for full sexual expression.

God says I should wait.

I don't want to get a girl pregnant.

I want sex to be very special.

I would have no respect for myself if I did it.

Sex before marriage is damaging.

The Bible says sex before marriage is wrong.

I'm afraid I may catch a serious disease.

Others may find out what I have done.

If I did have sex I would feel very guilty.

My virginity will be my best wedding gift to my wife.

I would hurt my spiritual life.

I only want to have sex with the person I marry.

before marriage means that the act that is supposed to bond man and woman together can become just something casual. The height of sexual ecstasy, that is, part of being 'one flesh', turns into something far less. For sex to be right, it has to be in the situation that God has said. Anything less is incomplete and can lead to sex being devalued. After all, if you sleep together before you're married, then what's to say that you may view sex as being not that significant after marriage?

Sex before marriage can easily become a habit; expected and not that important. Previous experience means that husband and wife no longer have that innocent exploration of sexuality together, that journey into the exciting unknown. Instead this may be replaced with an appetite for variety in ways that are not compatible with a Christian marriage.

Trust is damaged by sex before marriage; if you were willing to do that, what is the assurance you won't break other 'rules' after marriage. Surveys also reveal that sex before marriage means sex outside marriage is more likely — for both partners.

The feelings of guilt that often come from premarital sex may continue long into a marriage. Sex has enough wrong associations already, without you making it worse by adding guilt through foolish actions. And that's if marriage does follow

sex. What if it doesn't? What if both husband and wife have had previous sex partners? Such memories are painful and damaging to the marriage, and we know of too many cases in which memories of previous sexual partners have caused a marriage to fail.

Add to this the problem that sex before marriage blurs love. 'Is it really love?' you may ask yourself. Well, if you've already slept together, then how do you decide? You've already made the ultimate commitment without being committed! Sex in this way fools you into thinking that love is sex, or that some foolish infatuation is the real thing.

☐ *Social reasons.* Sex before marriage may be more acceptable today in some societies than before. But there's still the fact that reputations can be damaged. If you are a Christian, and it is revealed that you have had premarital sex, what is the likely reaction? What about respect for the other person and yourself? Sex alters the way you relate, not just to your sexual partner, but to many others. This is a surprise to many people. But think about marriage. Why is it a public ceremony? Because others in society have a part in your relationship together, and have to relate to the happy couple in a new way.

Sleep with a girl before marriage, and what does her family think? Your family? What about all the social customs which are there to make sure all is done in a proper

If the girl who you really want as a partner did an analysis of your lifestyle would it damage trust, the 'glue' that will hold you together?

and not even know. If you have been sexually active before, you may be giving the person you love most in the world a death sentence. Remember that AIDS can lie dormant in the body for ten years. You wouldn't even be aware of it . . . .

Sexually-transmitted diseases are not to be joked about. They can do much damage, and can be fatal. And it may not be just you who suffers. What about your future sexual partners? What about any children you might have that may also become infected? For the effects of such diseases are not limited to the 'guilty'; they can affect the innocent. Who wants that on their conscience?

The other major 'medical' result of sex is a baby! Are you ready to take responsibility for bringing another person into this world? Whatever contraception you may use is not absolutely guaranteed, and if you don't use anything at all, then you are either mad or a fool. Can you honestly say you are ready to be a parent, with all the duties involved? Or don't you care?

☐ *Spiritual reasons.* Most important of all for the Christian is the fact that sex before marriage damages your relationship with God. We have never met anyone who could prove differently. Some people deny it, but their life-styles say otherwise. Sex outside of God's plan is always a mistake. That's not to say it is the unforgivable sin, but it causes damage nevertheless.

Notice these clear commands:

way? What happens when you just think of your own pleasure?
☐ *Medical reasons.* Later on we'll consider casual sex and its health consequences. But for the moment remind yourself of AIDS and other diseases. You may contract a disease,

Part of sexual activity is to produce children and they have the right to be part of a secure, loving family. Are you ready to provide it?

'The body is not to be used for sexual immorality, but to serve the Lord.' 'Since you are God's people, it is not right that any matters of sexual immorality or indecency or greed should even be mentioned among you.' 'God wants you to be holy and completely free from sexual immorality.' (1 Corinthians 6:13; Ephesians 5:3; 1 Thessalonians 4:3.)

Why should God speak this way if sex before marriage was unimportant? If sexual immorality was no real problem? No: it is *because* of all the trouble such sex causes that God spells it out. And the reason given to the sexually-addicted Corinthians was: 'You know that your bodies are part of the body of Christ. Shall I take a part of Christ's body and make it part of the body of a prostitute? Impossible! Or perhaps you don't know that the man who joins his body to a prostitute becomes physically one with her? The scripture says quite plainly, "The two will become one body." ' (1 Corinthians 6:15, 16.)

Now you might argue that you are not planning to have sex with a prostitute but someone you say you love. But the same principle of being 'one body' together applies. How can you become 'one body' with someone you are not completely committed to? How can you say this is right for you when you have not decided to make your lives together? For sex is truly making love, a creative experience that involves the God of love — not just the transfer of bodily fluids.

☐ *Why wait? Why **not** wait?* For all these reasons, don't just think of your own immediate desires, but of all the implications. And decide beforehand, before you get into an impossible situation!

In all of this, remember that God truly is on your side. When the theory seems so distant, and the immediate situation so attractive, think of all God's good advice. He wants the best for you. Why should you doubt it? Take time to read again the practical suggestions for avoiding falling into temptation. For to make the right choice beforehand is so much better than having to deal with the consequences after.

QUESTIONS AND ANSWERS

Why does God make something so good so difficult to have?

Not because He's trying to tempt you. Remember it is our sinful nature and the Devil that tempts us, not God. Were Adam and Eve worried about sexual temptation? No, because they knew that God had made them for each other, and that all He made (including sex) was good. The problem is sin. The results of evil have affected all of us so that this wonderful experience of sexual love that God gave us has been perverted and distorted. Because of this, and the fact that sex is such a powerful force, means that the temptation to misuse sex can be very great. But no good comes of giving in to sexual temptations. Only by protecting and preserving sex as a sacred gift can it be as wonderful as God intended — the glorious and ultimate expression of human love within the marriage relationship.

Isn't the idea of waiting until marriage for sex out of date?

No. Just because many people do something doesn't make it good and right. And to say that sex before marriage is a modern invention is very foolish! Many of the young people we've spoken to are so grateful that they did wait until marriage for sex. They say it has brought them very close together, and because they know this was the first time for both of them they have no guilt or regrets. Ask yourself: who stands to gain from pushing the idea that sex before marriage is OK? Certainly not those who have done it! The wise words of the Bible are still true today, and we ignore them at our peril.

Just having a piece of paper doesn't really matter. What's important is being married in God's sight.

What actually makes you married then? The paper, the ring, the ceremony? If you think about it, none of these things sum up being married. What really counts are the vows (promises) you make to each other about having only each other and giving up anyone else. You say this not just before the witnesses present, but before God. And you also agree that this special relationship is to last your lifetimes. The question *you* ask makes marriage much less than that; and if a couple were only kept together by a piece of paper, then we doubt whether the marriage would last anyway. Being married involves all these things, including the 'civil contract' and that everyone around sees you now not as two single people, but as a married couple. You can't get rid of marriage that easily, especially not with a pious reference to being 'married in God's sight'!

Why did God make me this way?

What way? We presume you're referring to your sexuality. If so,

Don't let anyone tell you marriage is outmoded. It's still popular among those who want to make a public commitment of their promise to one another.

then we can only guess what your problem is. Sometimes people use this argument to excuse themselves: 'I can't help myself because God made me this way.' That's a way of avoiding responsibility and we can't accept that. But if you are struggling with some sexual problem then don't blame God. Ask for His help in dealing with it. Now there's nothing wrong with having sexual thoughts. If that's your problem, you need to accept your sexuality and make sure it is wholesome and good. But if you know that you are not right, then go back over what we've been

saying and, with God's help, find forgiveness and healing.

How far is too far?

If you're asking the question to justify what you already do, then think again! But if you are innocent, then we would say that you should not go beyond the counsel of God and the Bible. Immorality is more than physical matters anyway — it is an attitude of mind that seeks its own pleasure (often at the expense of others). But if you want a physical line, then we certainly believe that genital contact means it's hard not to go a lot further. So spend time in the romance of courtship, of hugs and kisses and holding hands. For as the physical involvement develops, it also accelerates. Make sure your conscience is clear, and that you are not fooling yourself either. Remember that substitute sex (oral sex, mutual masturbation, etc) can also bring guilt. It's not just full sexual intercourse that God warns against. Any sexual activity that ought to be reserved for marriage alone is 'too far'.

Some people have a long courtship relationship. Can this lead to sex outside of marriage?

As always, it depends. Depends on you and her. For some, the question doesn't arise, since even a short courtship ends up in sex before marriage. But because of our sexual makeup, there are practical difficulties in extending the courtship process. As we've seen, the human sexual response develops over the duration of a relationship. The drive is to go further every time you meet. So by putting off a decision for marriage, or making the date way off in the future, you will experience temptations that for some become increasingly difficult to withstand. This also depends on your previous experience, your sex drive and the attitude your partner takes. But even with the best will in the world from both sides, a long-extended physical relationship (kissing, cuddling, petting) without sex is hard to maintain, and so make sure you make the right decisions about when you marry. Better experience the problems of marriage (even when they're inconvenient for your career or whatever) than the problems of premarital sex.

What is the ideal courtship and marriage?

There isn't one! What works for one couple may be boring or stupid or weird for another. The combination of events, reactions and experiences that make up a courtship are special because of the person you're with.

Of course, some may want to define the ideal: boy meets girl, they fall in love, they marry, they live happily ever after. But we're in a real world, with real problems. The ideal is to be the best person you can be, with God's help. The ideal is not to compromise your principles. The ideal is to find someone who shares your beliefs about the really fundamental aspects of life. The ideal courtship and marriage has God at its centre.

Why is it important to be a virgin before you get married?

Sometimes the subject of virginity is approached with the idea of the male wanting to possess the best, not wanting 'damaged goods' and so on. Such ideas go back to times when women were virtually sold into marriage and became the man's possession. Such arguments are hardly Christian, and should not be part of any reasoning today.

Yet virginity — for both man and woman — is still God's ideal. Your first sexual experience is designed to be memorable, both physically and mentally. You need to show love and tenderness, you need more than plain sexual passion. Your gift of virginity is linked with the giving of yourself in the ultimate way. You are special, and you don't want your most complete sexual experience to be anything but special either. Your first time will be the beginning of a long, and we hope happy, sexual journey with your wife. No guilt. No second thoughts. No doubts. No regrets. No past to be anxious over, just a future life together.

9

When it all goes wrong

Flee from sexual immorality. All other sins a man commits are outside his body, but he who sins sexually sins against his own body. 1 Corinthians 6:18, NIV.

LESS THAN PERFECT

In a survey of Christian young people, problems related to sexuality scored very high as factors which affected their lives and their relationship to God. Of those who had indulged in premarital sex, over 90 per cent said they had experienced feelings of guilt. And from the seminars we've conducted, sexual problems clearly are a major source of sadness, shame and low self-worth.

Perhaps the most important statement to make is that we are all less than perfect. That's not to condone any kind of sin, sexual or otherwise. It's a simple statement of fact. And it is also a fact that a massive majority of Christians have struggled with some kind of sexual sin in their lives. Again that does not make sin 'acceptable', but it does tell you that you are not alone in your struggles.

The struggles vary. But all have at their heart a misdirection of the sex-ual drive God gave each of us. In this chapter we shall look at some of these different sexual behaviours and where they lead, thinking particularly of the situation before marriage. For we need to repeat again that *within* marriage is a very different situation to *before* marriage, and different rules apply. God does not condemn sexual exploration and enjoyment within marriage.

We have already identified sexual intercourse before marriage as not permissible for Christians. The Bible is very explicit on this point and, whatever people may say, this is an absolute. (If you have already gone too far, and this advice is too late, you will need to look carefully at chapters 12 and 13.) So with that position as our Christian baseline, what of other sexual practices that come close to sexual intercourse?

For though the Bible does not speak of them, there are basic principles of Christian behaviour which give us a good basis from which to proceed.

So let's deal with some of the danger zones of sexuality, particularly from the male perspective.

VISUAL STIMULATION

One of the saddest consequences of sin is that we are no longer able to relate to one another as complete persons. The exploitation of each by the other is a result of the selfishness at the heart of evil.

Think of the description of Adam and Eve before the Fall. They were naked and unashamed. Only after they broke their relationship with God did such shame at nakedness arise. They could no longer see each other as persons, but saw the physical bodies and were ashamed. So for us today, revealing the body is equated with sexual signals. We do not see the person under the skin, we just stop at the skin and the physical body. So much so that for some a woman may simply be a collection of body parts.

That is why we've headed this section 'visual stimulation'. Many aspects of male sexuality are involved here. You may be attracted by a shapely body, or some particular part of the female form. Now sexual attraction is not wrong. But when all you see is the body part, and not the whole person, you have problems. Male sexuality is particularly sensitive in this area. You may have been surprised the first time you were attracted in this way, and won-

dered why your body reacted as it did. This is not wrong. But when such sexual attraction gets out of control and turns to lust, then temptation and sin enter in.

So while you may admire beauty, make sure you are not looking 'with lust in your eyes' as Jesus said (see Matthew 5:28, Living Bible). Lust means seeing the other not as a person to be related to, but an object to satisfy your sexual drive. You may lust after watching a woman naked (as David did when watching Bathsheba bathing), in some alluring swimsuit, or even totally dressed. Only you know when your thoughts have passed the boundaries of decency and Christian principle. So guard what you see and the way you see it!

The shame that Adam and Eve felt for each other's nakedness was a result of sin; sin that is selfishness. Especially for the man, a naked woman can be an instant sexual signal. This same identification of nakedness with sexual attraction is the reason for pornography. The initial interest may be curiosity (to see what is under the clothes), but this is soon replaced with excitement at the sexual feeling induced by nakedness. Added to this is the 'forbidden fruit' aspect; the thrill at doing 'something naughty'.

Clothes are able to change completely a girl's image. No doubt too they can change your ideas about that girl. Clothes can tell you something about her personality but should you respond to more than physical attraction?

The tragedy is that pornography empties sex of its true meaning and enjoyment, replacing it with mechanical and lifeless pictures. Sex is made trivial and, to be honest, dull. The sex act portrayed just as bodies joining is truly uninteresting and boring. The true thrill of sexual union is in the joining of the minds, not the crude copulation of some figures on a page or on some flickering screen.

Man's exploitation of woman by trying either to extract her sexuality and market it in plastic bags, or by making her some kind of goddess figure (or Miss World, or Playmate, whatever) results in taking away the reality of individual women. Whether it was the Canaanite cult prostitute or the modern-day porn star, sex is abused and perverted into a mistaken way of relating to the female kind.

The truth is that no woman is always 'hot for sex' or 'ready to fulfil your deepest fantasies' as pornography proclaims. Real women have work to do, family pressures, periods, studies, friends to see; and, most important, their own sexual desires and wishes. Only by seeing women as real persons can any relationship be meaningful and successful.

It is inexcusable to treat a woman as an object. They too have feelings of fun and despair, they suffer from pressure, they have needs, hopes and desires, and they have to suffer men's distorted views of women.

ORAL AND MUTUAL MASTURBATION

The Bible is silent about both oral sex and mutual masturbation as practices, but that does not mean it has nothing to say about sexual principles. It does refer to lust and improper sexual conduct, so we can make some deductions as to Christian behaviour. Oral sex is sometimes seen as part of a 'natural progression' of kissing (since it involves sucking and kissing each others' genitals). But we would argue that this is not necessarily true, and is far more like sex that should be reserved for marriage. Similarly mutual masturbation (where one partner manipulates the others genitals by hand to achieve orgasm) is another sex substitute that would seem to have more in common with the full sexual expression of marriage than an appropriate activity for a girl and boy 'just going out together'.

Although couples often suggest to us that these sexual 'alternatives' are 'better' than doing 'it' and so should be seen at least as the lesser of the evils, is this really true? The argument that a girl stimulates her boy-friend to orgasm with her hand is acceptable since it means they are not having sex shows how easily we can deceive our consciences. It may mean that the girl doesn't get pregnant, or that diseases are not spread. But we

ON DECEIVING YOURSELF

Check out these statements to see if you have thought this way and if you are deceiving yourself. Tick those that apply, and then think about what this means for you personally:

- Girls can be a tease and sometimes you have to show them who is boss with a bit of force.

- If you've spent money on a girl, then she owes you some sexual favours.

- If a girl dresses sexily she deserves all she gets.

- You prove yourself a man by treating a woman rough.

- It's OK to have sex with a girl if she's got you so turned on you can't stop.

- Looking at pictures of naked girls is normal so it's not really wrong.

- There's no problem in looking as long as you don't touch.

- At least oral sex means you're not breaking the commandments.

- Masturbation means you don't go out and rape someone so it must be OK.

- When a girl says no to you when you want sex, she really means yes.

All these statements have been used by men to justify themselves. All of them are untrue in some way. Look again and see if you have not been guilty of thinking in this way at times.

believe that such sexual activity is still sex (and by the way, some diseases can still be spread by oral sex, like gonorrhoea).

Is it really true that the boy is so incapable of controlling himself that he has to have some kind of relief? This suggests that the male has to have sex and continues the myth of having to 'slake his lust'. This is not an acceptable conclusion to any respectable man, nor is it biblical.

Do these practices really help? Although they can be viewed as preventing something worse, this does not make them right and good. If you demand such practices from your girl-friend, what does this say about the way you see your relationship, not only now, but in the future? And what does she think of you for wanting to be satisfied in this way?

From a Christian perspective, what does love say about this? Not seeking its own selfish pleasure, thinking of the other, not delighting in evil and so on? If all we want is physical gratification, what does that say about our spiritual condition? While God does not look to condemn us, He does wish much more for our sexual behaviour than a quick bit of stimulation to take care of an urge. And even if it is mutual, we know that many who have used such sex substitutes have experienced similar guilt to those who have had sexual intercourse.

Don't be satisfied with second-best is our advice. Enjoy the completeness in marriage, and while we would not condemn you, seek to return to a good and healthy and guiltless relationship with your girl-friend so that you can be happy in each others' love.

MASTURBATION

Similar thoughts apply when we are asked about masturbation. Just because it is a common practice does not make it good. Drinking and smoking may be common — that does not make them good for you! Let's list the arguments for and against:

For:
Everybody does it — so it's OK
God never said it was wrong
It's a way of taking care of sexual pressures
You can tune into your own sexuality
It's good practice for the real thing
Against:
It's second-rate. Sex was meant for two, not one
Instead of sharing you're being selfish
Sex on your own can become an obsessive habit
Sexual fantasies go against Bible principles
The real thing may not be as good as your fantasies

In a survey of Christian males, 94 per cent admitted to masturbation, with 90 per cent feeling guilty about having done it. This indicates two important factors. Firstly, masturbation is a common practice (though we must always be clear that the majority is not always right!). Because of this, the Church must take it seriously and seek to provide helpful advice and information. The old warnings that masturbation destroyed the brain or made you blind cannot be supported. Such scare tactics only make things worse, and confuse the issue.

But neither can we agree with the current thought that masturbation is totally harmless and should even be encouraged. The danger of masturbation becoming an obsessive habit is a very real one, and can continue into marriage with damaging results. If you have discovered that masturbation does bring physical pleasure, then it is hard to avoid repeating the experience. Together with the act come mental fantasies which may go well beyond Christian morality. Often (especially in the case of male masturbation) erotic or pornographic material is used as a visual stimulus for masturbation. Quite obviously this cannot be seen as helpful from the Christian perspective.

But in dealing with masturbation it's vital to distinguish any guilt feelings for the action from sex as a whole. All too many have grown up with masturbation to believe that all sex is dirty and wrong. From bad advice that has called masturbation perverted and filthy comes the idea that every aspect of human sexuality is also perverted and filthy. In this way severe damage can be caused that is hard to cure. In all our discussions of our sexuality, we must always remember that God made it good. Sex is not perverted and filthy when it is in the context that God gave it, and just because you have masturbated at some time does not make you a sexual pervert. Many grow through the masturbation stage and have a well-balanced and fulfilled sexual relationship in marriage.

All of that said, we would want to make it clear that we do believe masturbation is less than ideal. Why? Because it is a denial of the truth that sex was intended to be between *two*, not one on his or her own. Where is the self-giving, sharing and caring aspects of sex in masturbation? It is basically selfish, looking to satisfy your own sexual urges. Masturbation is turning your sexual expression in on yourself, not sharing it with another in a loving way. In that sense then masturbation does question God's original intention since He otherwise would have made only one, not two human beings!

Of course, if it is to be argued which is better, to masturbate or to go out and rape or abuse or commit some other sexual crime, then it must be a lesser 'evil'. If masturbation is only the release of 'tension' or for the provision of a semen sample, it is hard to identify that as wrong. But, as Jesus made clear, it is what is happening in your head that is the important question. And only you can say what you are thinking of. As the Bible advises, whatsoever things are pure, honest, of good report . . . think on these things.

If you do believe that masturbation is a problem for you, especially if it happens frequently, then you will want to consider some advice. The old ideas about going and taking a cold shower are not that helpful! Nor is the counsel to make yourself really tired, by playing a lot of sports, for example. This may

It is important to find diversions, don't let your mind go into idle mode, read a book, pursue a hobby, become more social, widen your interests.

take away your energy, but you also know that when you are tired it's easier to give in to a particular habit. So a few suggestions:

☐ Control your fantasies. Masturbation is often associated with particular fantasies that appeal to you. So they need to be changed, and not concentrated on. Do not feed your mind with images and ideas that strengthen these fantasies, but rather choose other ideas.

☐ Make sure your mind is occupied with other things. And don't get too worried about masturbation, for the more you think about it, the harder it gets to avoid the practice. So make sure you have plenty to do, and if masturbation is a late night activity then either read a book or enjoy some hobby before you go to sleep.

☐ Make friends and become more social. Masturbation is frequently part of loneliness, and is a way to handle your need for intimate love. We're not saying you should rush out and find the nearest girl to start a relationship with as a cure for masturbation. But it is important to have close friends with whom you can find love and appreciation. You cannot look to yourself to meet your own emotional needs, for if you do this you can become very self-centred.

☐ As some guys said at a seminar: 'Get a life!' Masturbation can be associated with lack of ambition and satisfaction with your life-situation. You need to take control of your life and do something positive to achieve your dreams. While progress may be slow, don't feel a failure, since this feeds your need to satisfy yourself sexually at least. And remember that most do pass through the masturbation stage to a mature and fulfilled sexual experience within marriage.

SEX

The principles on which Christians should act

Sex is good.
GENESIS 2:18-25.

Sex has consequences.
GALATIANS 6:7, 8; ROMANS 1:24, 25.

Sex must not control you.
1 THESSALONIANS 4:4, 5;
1 CORINTHIANS 6:12-14; 10:23, 24.

Sex is secondary to love.
1 CORINTHIANS 13:1-13.

Sex can sometimes only be handled by running.
GENESIS 39:12.

Sex becomes more dangerous as you mess around with it.
JAMES 1:12-15; 1 THESSALONIANS 4:3-8.

Sex is a great temptation, but it can be resisted.
1 CORINTHAINS 10:13.

Sex is two becoming one.
GENESIS 2:24; MATTHEW 19:5;
1 CORINTHIANS 6:16.

Sex must honour God.
1 CORINTHIANS 6:20.

Sex is designed to be the completion of intimacy.
GENESIS 2:23, 24.

RAPE

'I didn't mean to.'

'She wanted it as much as me.'

'I never forced her anyway.'

'I lost control.'

'She was really asking for it.'

When it comes to agreement in sexual relationships you, as a single male, need to be aware of possible problems. The cry of 'rape' is heard frequently, and needs to be addressed.

You may say, 'I'd never force anyone. I couldn't rape.' However, others have also said the same and ended up raping. So-called 'date rape' is a very real problem. Alternatively you may believe you have both agreed to sex — and then discover that you are charged with rape when she becomes remorseful afterwards. Or you may have done nothing, and yet still be falsely accused.

Tragedies whatever the rights and wrongs of any particular case. In the news this week are two very different stories.

One involves a young man who was accused of rape, and acquitted since there was no evidence whatsoever of the violence claimed ever having happened. (The girl said she was hit and her clothes ripped from her. No bruising was found by the police doctor, and no ripped clothing was ever produced.) Even though he was found not guilty, he had been identified in the papers as 'a rapist'. His supposed victim could not be named due to the legal rules regarding rape, but he was. And so,

at the age of 22, he went home and hanged himself.

The other case is of a girl who accepted a ride home in a car containing four men. Instead of taking her home they took her to an unused garage and took turns in raping her, and then left her injured and naked to crawl away for help. Despite the clear evidence of rape, and the terrible trauma the girl had experienced, when it came to making a statement and accusing the men involved she became frightened and refused to lay charges. It seems that she was threatened with further violence if she took any kind of legal action. Without her co-operation, the police had no case.

Both these cases, and many others, make us angry. Angry because of the hurt and pain involved. Angry because of injustices caused. But angry most of all that God's great gift of loving tenderness between a man and a woman to bring them intimately close should become a weapon of violence used to separate viciously.

Add to that the frequency of rape. Only a small percentage of rapes are reported — for many reasons. The girl may feel threatened, or guilty herself, or unwilling to add to her pain by reliving the incident. She may wish to deny it, or to hide from possible public censure.

Or, as noted above, rape may be used as a threat to control the man, or to punish even though he may have done nothing. Joseph's imprisonment for supposedly raping Potiphar's wife may have happened more than 4,000 years ago, but the same situation still occurs today.

So even 'consent' to sexual intercourse can be fraught with danger, and illustrates once again how sex **must** be part of a loving, trusting relationship. Arguments over who said what to whom, whether consent was explicit or implied, and what actually took place usually end up being the boy's word against the girl's, since there are rarely any witnesses.

As a case study in how rape can happen as a result of bad sexual fantasies, you only have to look at the biblical description of Amnon and Tamar (2 Samuel 13).

From the beginning of the story it's clear that Amnon had become infatuated with his half-sister Tamar. He had even become sick because of this obsession, which he put down to being 'in love'. But this was far from true love.

Enter a scheming friend who suggested to Amnon that he fake sickness and ask Tamar to be sent to look after him. Then when they were alone Amnon grabbed hold of her and ordered her to come to bed with him. Such a trap is obviously not the way of love and morality. And despite Tamar's wise words about his foolishness,

'He refused to listen to her, and since he was stronger than she, he raped her. Then Amnon hated her with intense hatred. In fact, he hated

A rapist uses his victim as an object to gratify his own selfish indulgence yet the girl is left traumatized and abused, sometimes for life.

her more than he had loved her. Amnon said to her, "Get up and get out!"' (2 Samuel 13:14, 15, NIV.)

See how such sexual violence destroys the very basis of love. The real evil of rape is that it turns God's gift of loving trust and consent into violent force. Because Amnon allowed his foolish fantasies to take control of his actions, his obsession turned to lust. Then his lust was dwelt on until actions replaced the images, and rape was the result. Not only that, but once he had forced Tamar, he then found

It is sad when God's great gift of loving tenderness between a man and woman becomes a weapon of violence.

his 'love' never existed, and he hated her instead. A series of sins that led from one to another, with catastrophic results. Tamar's rape was discovered by Absolom, who arranged Amnon's murder, and who eventually rebelled against his father David. The end result was many deaths, including that of Absolom himself. A sorry catalogue of evil that was triggered by the immoral lusts of Amnon.

Remember: rape is to be seen in the same light as murder, for it is an action that destroys personality and kills life. Whatever the circumstances, *never ever* believe that the use of force in sex is justified.

QUESTIONS AND ANSWERS

What is the Christian view of oral sex?

As we've said, there is no mention in the Bible of this sexual practice. But that doesn't mean that there are no principles that can guide us here. Christians may be divided on its appropriateness, but since it can have a similar result to sexual intercourse (orgasm and ejaculation) then it must be treated similarly. Sadly some unmarried Christian couples have believed that only sexual intercourse is 'banned' and so any other sexual activity is acceptable. Oral sex is used in this way to gain satisfaction and relieve sexual tension. But this does not say that simply because the penis has not penetrated the vagina then 'God doesn't mind'. Our conviction is that sexual activity that involves genital contact is not healthy for an unmarried Christian couple.

What's really wrong with playing with yourself? I find I really can't stop anyway.

If you mean masturbation then you need to look at what this is doing to your life. Masturbation can become very compulsive, especially among boys. It is both physically and mentally draining, and can badly affect your spiritual life. Just because modern society says it won't hurt you doesn't mean you have to follow along with such an idea. Is it really true that God made you with a drive that you can't control? And

what about sex as a wonderful gift of one to the other? You are only relating to yourself, which is less than the ideal that God created. Also masturbation may not reduce your sexual tension, but increase your sexual frustration.

Would you say masturbation is a sin?

We cannot go beyond what God has said, and because He has not specifically spoken about masturbation we would not wish to state categorically that it is a definite sin. But as always there are circumstances that will show you that masturbation may be unhelpful in dealing with your sexuality. We would say that it is less than the best that God intended. It is solo-sex that turns you in on yourself. And if masturbation is getting in the way of your relationship with God then you need to deal with it realistically.

My girl-friend was raped once before I met her, and now she really doesn't want any kind of physical contact. What should I do?

A tragic question. All we can say is that you need to talk about the situation together, and perhaps also with a trained counsellor. Your girl-friend needs to find healing from the mental scars, which includes the need to be happy touching again. In some cases of rape, there is a fear of intercourse afterwards. In other cases, the girl feels she is already 'used' and becomes promiscuous. You need to be particularly sensitive to her situation and her needs, and not force the pace of intimacy. You could suggest that she takes the lead so that she can decide what level of touching she is comfortable with. If she feels she is in control it may help her not to become anxious about the situation. But you both need more help than we can give here.

I worry about how much I think about sex. Sometimes my fantasies are quite rough. Do you think I could get carried away and do something to a girl that was wrong?

If you mean you fear you could be violent sexually, or force a girl to do something against her will, then you need counselling. You may simply be worrying overmuch though, since teenage boys do think about sex a great deal, and this does not mean you are necessarily a pervert or a potential rapist. But we would advise you to speak to a mature counsellor who can help you work out your thoughts and feelings, especially any violent fantasies, and if you do see yourself getting out of control, seek help quickly.

Why does the church say premarital sex is wrong? Isn't that just part of the way people used to be controlled by society?

Don't believe all that nonsense that says the church is just an agent of social control, and so all its beliefs should be abandoned. While the church may not have always acted from pure motives, the idea that teachings against premarital sex are just ways of promoting control is dangerous foolishness. The reason premarital sex is wrong is because of the damage is does, not primarily to society, but to you and your sexual partner(s).

How does God feel about me now that I've done it?

This question was asked during a counselling session and shows the thought that 'Now God has to treat me as a real sinner.' Of course you need to take the situation seriously. Premarital sex cannot be termed a 'good idea'. But don't make the opposite mistake and think that this is the unforgivable sin, and that God hides His face from you. You need to reject the idea that since you've done something wrong God can't help you. In fact you need God now more than ever. Tell Him exactly what you think and feel, ask for His forgiveness and accept the gracious mercy only He can give. And as Jesus said, 'Go and sin no more'!

Why doesn't God take away my desire for masturbation?

God does not force anyone even if they ask, nor does He take away the temptation. But the Bible is clear that He does give strength to resist sinful desires, and if you know your masturbation involves immoral fantasies and so on then He surely can help.

It is important to confront your sin, to admit guilt and to offload it onto a God who, thankfully, never shuts the door on you.

10

Sexual distortions

What human nature does is quite plain. It shows itself in immoral, filthy and indecent actions. Galatians 5:19.

OBSESSIVE SEX

Richard called and asked for an appointment. 'It may take some time,' he warned. So a meeting was scheduled for one afternoon. He came in the room in obvious distress.

'I really don't know where to start,' he confessed.

But after a few failed attempts, the whole story came tumbling out. How he'd become controlled by his sexual drive in his early teens through some sad experiences, introduced to hard-core pornography by older boys, rejected by girl after girl in his search for love and companionship, told by his 'friends' to view women as just things of pleasure, and so on.

There had been a series of complications in Richard's life which seemed to have compounded his problem. The family had moved frequently, meaning he had not had the opportunity to develop really close friendships with either boys or girls. He had not been able to speak with his parents about sexual matters. And he had come to believe that sex and religion had nothing in common whatsoever.

The result was the development of sexually-obsessive behaviour. He'd spend many hours each day in his sexual fantasies, many of which he'd developed from pornographic stories and so had little truth or reality as their base. For in his dreams every girl was a sex-crazed slut who wanted to be dominated and sexually abused. He desired girls simply as tools to fulfil his lusts. He conquered as a sexual hero and then moved on. Because, in reality, this wasn't so (and could never be so) Richard became lonely and withdrawn, and devoted even more time to his fantasy sex. So much so that all other aspects of his life suffered — his studies, his relationship with family and friends, his health.

'I know I have to stop but I just can't,' he said in a voice broken with emotion. 'Sex is a monster inside me, eating me from within. And I'm afraid of what it might make me do.'

For he had already tried to make those girls he'd dated fit his dream models. That was probably why he had experienced so much rejection. If the sexual distortions he'd acquired were not corrected, it was easy to see how his obsessions could eventually end in sexual violence and crime.

Like a drug, sex can be abused. Richard showed many signs of sexual addiction: frequent masturbation, heavy use of pornography, many hours spent in sexual fantasies, unreal expectations of and from women, serious impact on lifestyle and behaviour, low self-esteem and major mood swings, a self-destructive attitude and lack of real concern over adverse consequences of his obsessive actions.

How could a Christian ever become like this? That was the question Richard had asked himself so often. Like most difficult sexual problems, it had a number of causes. Some were the results of his own choices, others related to his personal circumstances. But the end result was a person with severe sexual problems, acutely aware of how out-of-line his practices were with Scripture and yet, seemingly, unable to do anything about them. 'I feel like I'm swept along on a sexual tide and I just can't swim against it. I've tried so often, but every time I've failed. I can't see how God could ever love someone so sunk in sin as me.'

Because sex addiction comes so close to who you are, it is extremely difficult for the sex addict to alter his behaviour. That is why qualified help is so important, realizing that this tragic addiction is far more common than most people think. It

Personal sexual abuse can do much damage to your life-style, your social life and your studies.

is estimated, for example, that there are between nine and fifteen million sex addicts in the US alone.

Together with Richard, we laid the Christian foundation for his recovery; understanding that sex *is* good, that God is very much involved in creating and sustaining the sexual drive, that rightly understood and expressed sexual activity can be tremendously meaningful and fulfilling. Then we looked at what he was doing to himself, the lack of self-value, the evil actions he was carrying out *against himself*. For it does not help to say that sin is not sin. Sexual addiction is far from God's intention for us, and is an aspect of sin and evil.

But neither is it so vile that there is no redemption. We then saw how God can help and heal, and that there is a way back to God and goodness through His grace. Together with medical help and professional therapy, Richard is on his way back to becoming a whole person once more, not just a slave to his sexual fantasies.

So what is 'normal' and what is 'obsessive'? Guys frequently worry about how normal they are, because they may often have sexual dreams and fantasies. The truth is that in the teen years thinking about sex (even very often) is quite normal. Part of the process of development, sexual awareness brings many questions and thoughts, and *it is not a sin to have sexual thoughts*.

But because of the sexually-saturated world in which we live, it's important to guard 'the avenues of the soul'; the mental and spiritual food we put into our minds. As one computer proverb says, 'Garbage in, garbage out.' If you put rubbish into your mind, you must not be surprised if all you get out is rubbish too. This is particularly true of sexual images that would be termed pornography.

A rubbish bin is a better recepticle than your mind for sexually-depraving material.

PORNOGRAPHY

We've already looked at visual signals and how most men are very turned on by sexual images. That in itself may not be wrong, in the right setting. For a husband to be sexually excited by seeing his wife undressed is normal and natural, and part of the way God has made us. But to use that visual stimulation to fill the mind with lust is very unhealthy. Many men have had their lives ruined by an addiction to pornography, and once the images are in the mind, they are hard to erase.

The architect of evil knows well the effect of pornography, and uses this to wicked ends. It may begin relatively harmlessly, by looking at the underwear section of a shopping catalogue, as one young man admitted. But then this led to buying girlie magazines, and eventually to the need for even greater stimulation through hard-core pornography where every conceivable sexual act is displayed.

You see how there is a process involved here? Almost unnoticed, the user of pornography wants more and more, until he only finds satisfaction in the most perverse images. Such a result is common, and shows where even the first steps of the use of pornography lead.

Realizing this, no Christian can believe that pornography is helpful to his life or his relationship with God. What may begin as curiosity can end up as an addiction, where the pictures are valued more than even a real-life woman.

PROSTITUTION

'You know that your bodies are parts of the bodies of Christ. Shall I take a part of Christ's body and make it part of the body of a prostitute? Impossible! Or perhaps you don't know that the man who joins his body to a prostitute becomes physically one with her?' (1 Corinthians 6:15, 16.) Note that in this particular text the reason for not going to a prostitute is not given as a breaking of a commandment. Even more importantly than that is the reason that you are trying to join yourself as a Christian with an alien 'religion'. What link is there between Christ and the Devil? is the question asked elsewhere. There can be no possible link, there is no way that sexual pleasure with a prostitute can be any part of the Christian life. It is death to it — and will kill the spiritual experience you share with God. For as the text goes on, you are a dwelling place for the Spirit of God. So it is impossible to be both part of a body with a prostitute and use your body to become one with someone who is selling you sex.

But it is surprising how Christians do become tempted and fall into such temptation. Why? Because of the lure of sexual pleasure, to prove yourself a man, to satisfy curiosity perhaps. But remember how dangerous this is, physically and spiritually. It will be statistically likely that a prostitute has some sexually-transmitted disease. And the damage to your spiritual life can be devastating. So be wise, and follow Solomon's advice (see Proverbs 7) and avoid such immoral women.

And before we leave this subject, we need to record that Jesus did extend His salvation to those who were considered immoral women in His time. The reasons why a woman becomes a prostitute are often because of some evil done to them, often by men, perhaps when they were young girls. So before we accuse, let us remember that without clients there would be no prostitutes, and that they need care and concern too.

ABUSE

We do not intend to dwell on sexual abuse. But we do need to recognize that it does exist, and that some who have been abused grow up to become abusers themselves. While the sexual abuse of boys is statistically less frequent than the abuse of girls, it *does* happen and should be reported. If you have experienced sexual abuse, you need to experience recovery and healing. And if you are ever tempted to abuse, either a child or any other human being, remember that you are doing a very great wrong, an evil that can damage and destroy another's life. If you feel you cannot help yourself, then get help. Remember Jesus' words: "'If anyone should cause one of these little ones to lose his faith in me, it would

In one survey undertaken in Australia 18 per cent of the sample of youth aged 19-25 reported having been sexually abused, the majority of them female.

In a similar survey undertaken in Northern Europe 1 out of 12 young people had been sexually abused; 85 per cent females, 15 per cent males. 28 per cent had been abused by a close family member, 21 per cent by a relative or friend of the family.

be better for that person to have a large millstone tied round his neck and be drowned in the deep sea.'" (Matthew 18:6.)

SEXUAL PERVERSIONS

Surely one of the greatest tragedies is the ability human beings have to take God's great and beautiful gift of sexuality, and turn it into something terribly evil. Sexual perversions have been around for a long time, and have caused great damage to many, including the innocent. When sexual love is taken and made into something gross and disgusting, then we cease to be truly human. To say that we become like beasts is to defame animals, who would never act in the way that some who call themselves human do.

Before the Flood, God looked at the earth and saw the people there. It's recorded that He 'saw how wicked everyone on earth was and how evil their thoughts were all the time.' (Genesis 6:5.) Because human sinfulness, including sexual perversions, are similar today, then God must see us in a similar way. Sex used and abused: performed in an uncaring and totally physical way. A long way from what God wants and intends. As Jeremiah commented: 'The heart is deceitful above all things, and desperately wicked: who can know it?' Jeremiah 17:9, KJV.

How is it possible that God actually had to tell His people not to have sex with close relatives? What does it say when Leviticus 18-20 records that a man is not to have sexual relations with his mother, sister or granddaughter? Or not to make your daughter a prostitute? Or not to have sex with another man? Or not to have sex with an animal?

Because God took such perversions so seriously, because they were so damaging to individuals and society, they carried the death sentence. Look what had to happen to Sodom and Gomorrah. Sexual perversions are totally anti-God, because they take the heart out of sexual love and replace it with uncaring exploitation and abuse.

(Such perversions are rightly condemned. But sometimes people make other things perversions, for example saying that different sexual positions are sexual perversions. We would only comment that we must not go beyond what God has said, and that different sexual positions within marriage are certainly not perversions at all.)

The abuse of innocent children is an evil act which can damage and destroy their future lives.

HOMOSEXUALITY

Because so much nonsense is talked about the Bible's attitude to homosexual activity it's important to look at exactly what it does say:

'No man is to have sexual relations with another man; God hates that.' (Leviticus 18:22.)

'If a man has sexual relations with another man, they have done a disgusting thing, and both shall be put to death. They are responsible for their own death.' (Leviticus 20:13.)

'Do not fool yourselves; people who are immoral or who worship idols or are adulterers or homosexual perverts . . . — none of these will possess God's kingdom.' (1 Corinthians 6:9, 10.)

'They exchange the truth about God for a lie; they worship and serve what God has created instead of the Creator himself, who is to be praised forever! Amen. Because they do this, God has given them over to shameful passions. Even the women pervert the natural use of their sex by unnatural acts. In the same way the men give up natural sexual relations with women and burn with passion for each other. Men do shameful things with each other, and as a result they bring upon themselves the punishment they deserve for their wrongdoing' (Romans 1:25-27.)

Homosexuals have lobbied long and hard for their sexual habits to be accepted as natural human behaviour. But by biology alone it has to be seen as distorted and defective.

While we must be careful not to single out homosexuality as being the worst sin, it's clear from God's Word that the practice of homosexuality cannot be part of a Christian's experience. Much ongoing research is being carried out into the causes of and reasons behind homosexuality, and it may well be true that for some people the sexual attraction of the same sex may be very great. However, to suggest that 'God made me this way' is to deny the clear abhorrence of God for what He calls unnatural practices, and to suggest that homosexuals cannot change ignores the transforming power of God. To further suggest that 'It's OK to be gay' confuses the issue even more and leaves the homosexual even further away from God's healing of the damage of sin.

The idea that 'the best way to remove sin is to deny it' does not help. The hostility and anger of homosexual pressure groups, and the demands for homosexuality to be taught as an equally valid life-style calls to mind the arrogant and shameless attitudes of those in Rome addressed by Paul in the first century. Today 'The love that previously dared not speak its name has now grown hoarse from screaming it.' (Robert Brustein, *New York Times*, 22 November 1977.)

Liberty in sexuality is not a licence to slake lust, an outlook that says, 'I just please myself.' The *demand* for the acceptance of homosexual relationships, even within the Church, goes against the whole principle of love as outlined in 1 Corinthians 13 which explains that *by definition* love does not seek its own way.

Gay 'pride', campaigns to 'out' prominent people and make them confess their homosexuality, bishops who admit that they are gay or that their sexuality is a 'grey area' — all these aspects of our society suggest we have identified tolerance with compromise. While Christians cannot expect non-Christians to follow God's teachings, neither can they accept that what God has identified as wrong and unnatural has now become right and acceptable.

So what of the homosexual and his (assuming the male kind) problems? Is he to be dismissed as a pervert without the hope of salvation? Is he to be shunned as a source of sexual infection?

The variety of responses means we have to examine what should be the Christian's reaction to the person. And we must be slow to jump to conclusions. Sometimes teenage boys become convinced they are gay just because they like another boy. Older homosexuals may also attempt to influence others who are vulnerable. And the massive media exposure given to homosexuality raises the idea in many a boy's mind during the adolescent years when boys may be susceptible to such suggestions.

Like any other kind of sinner,

homosexuals are to be shown God's love and His acceptance of them as His children. Christians must speak in terms of acceptance of homosexuals *as persons*, not as devils or damned sinners. But in so doing the Church needs to repeat the principles of sexuality we have been dealing with here — and that homosexual behaviour is *not* consistent with a Christian life. To say anything else is to lie.

God's gift of sexuality is as part of the whole being. We cannot separate our sexuality from the rest of ourself. It is an essential part of our character, and this will be adversely affected by a distorted sexuality. Our sexuality needs to be focused outside of ourselves, and finds its fulfilment in the most intimate of human relationships. And finally, our sexuality as created by God leads us to find its highest expression in the loving, committed union of man and woman — which by definition must be heterosexual, not homosexual.

CONCLUSION

In all this we do not seek to condemn, but to redeem. God offers a way back from all sin, and if you are affected by anything we have discussed here, you need to read the last two chapters and find God's healing grace that can re-make you in His glorious image. But before you can accept this healing of sin's damage in your life, you have to accept your sinfulness, and want to be changed. Until then, nothing can happen. So if this applies to you, think about it.

The choice is before you.

MY ATTITUDE TO 'BROKEN SEX'

After you have considered whether these statements are true or false tick the appropriate box. You might find some hard to answer!

T F

☐ ☐ God is more against sexual sins than any others.

☐ ☐ The Church should not get involved in discussing sexual distortions.

☐ ☐ Sex can be addictive like a drug.

☐ ☐ Homosexuals are cursed by God.

☐ ☐ Pornography is a private matter and it's up to the individual.

☐ ☐ All nudity is evil.

☐ ☐ Even though it shouldn't, child abuse does happen within the Church.

☐ ☐ In dealing with people with sexual problems, we should still love them.

☐ ☐ Homosexuality is worse than other sexual sins because it goes against nature.

☐ ☐ It's not a sin to have sexual thoughts.

QUESTIONS AND ANSWERS

I find myself looking at girls in a way that gets me worried. How much sin is there in just looking?

In the same way as beauty is in the eye of the beholder, so is the right and wrong of looking. Some men look at women and see just certain 'parts'. (Some are attracted by big breasts, some like long legs, some the buttocks and so on.) But to reduce a woman to being just the total of body parts is to make her less than human. A woman who is only appreciated because of her body is not seen as a human being with whom you want a personal relationship. This is part of the way that sex has been used to reduce a wonderful mental, emotional and spiritual experience into just a joining of body parts. So: to look in itself is not wrong. But if the physical is all you see, then you are reducing yourself to the level of a machine. And if the only thing that is there is lust, then, as Jesus says, you might as well be blind since such an attitude will not help you or her.

What exactly is pornography? Is it just pictures of girls with no clothes on?

The literal meaning of pornography is 'the graphical depiction of whores'. In this sense then pornography covers all kinds of sexual descriptions that relate to prostitution. In other words, sex that is debased into some kind of 'business'. Not every picture of

Manufacturers are quite aware that for males the female body has potential sales appeal. At the same time it reduces a woman's value to that of the product.

nudity falls into this category; medical pictures, classical paintings and statues and so on. The basic point of pornography is deliberately to make people (usually men) sexually excited. This often leads to masturbation with such pictures (or films or even books). Computer porn and sex phone lines are used by some to stimulate fantasies. Such sexual fantasies are obviously a long way from God's best for human beings and can also damage later relationships. If you are tempted to satisfy your curiosity about such pornography, don't! It can become a habit that is hard to break, and it leads to a poor image of women since they are seen as under male control, only existing to satisfy male sexual desires.

The evil fantasies of pornography have been made worse since the advent of the video, the computer and the internet.

I find myself thinking about sex all the time. Everything I do is to try and seduce a woman. I just want sex and more sex. What should I do?

This question was not written down, but sums up what one young man told us as we talked. Sex had taken over his life. Somehow he had come to believe that sex was the answer to everything. We explained that sex was only part of what should be a loving, giving relationship and not a question of finding satisfaction and getting what he wanted. Almost like 'collecting' sexual experiences, he had thought that his sexual conquests were something to be proud of. When we explained that quite the contrary was the case and that we felt sorry for him, he began to see his attitude in a different light. He also needed to refocus his life away from this unhealthy preoccupation with sex, and see that there are many other areas that make up a balanced life. As we studied together, he discovered the meaning of love and intimate relationships as part of the divine creation. In a society that concentrates so much on sex, you really *do* need divine help to break out of this cycle — along with some good human counsellors.

What makes someone a homosexual?

No specific cause has been identified, which suggests that a number of factors are involved, not the least being the exercise of choice.

Despite previous claims by a homosexual research scientist to have discovered a 'gay gene', other scientists have not been able to reproduce his results. While aspects of heredity may cause some men to be more 'effeminate' than others, this is no cause for homosexuality. Links with hormonal levels (especially male hormone levels) have only produced negative or conflicting results. Other explanations, such as a poor relationship of the boy with his father, a dominant mother, or a generally bad family background, have not been found to be decisive, although some of these factors may be relevant. In the end, and although there may be contributing factors, we still believe that no one is made a homosexual or cannot be changed. Such ideas are in opposition to the Christian view of personal responsibility, and homosexuality cannot be excused by saying 'God made me that way' or 'I blame my parents'.

I think I'm homosexual. What should I do about it?

Ask yourself why you believe you are a homosexual. Many teenagers become convinced they are homosexual just because they happen to like a member of the

FOR YOUR DISCUSSION

Violent pornography has been shown to be related to rape. Rapists often admit to having used explicit sexual material that contains violence. What does that tell you, firstly, about the use of violent pornography and, secondly, the factors behind rape?

Homosexuality was common in Paul's day. So when he writes about sexual perverts in 1 Timothy 1:10 and about how men give up 'natural sexual relations with women and burn with passion for each other' (Romans 1:27) then how can it be argued that Paul does not condemn homosexual practice? Why do so many argue today that the Bible does not forbid homosexual behaviour?

Sexual abuse has become a high-profile issue in our modern world. How should a Christian respond, and what are the dangers? How can the Church get involved in this issue?

How do you think you could help someone who seemed to be obsessed by sex? What does the Bible say to help? Why is it important to have a balanced view of human sexuality?

What is the attraction of pornography? Why is it wrong? Is it 'the victimless crime'? How can someone who has fallen under its power be helped?

same sex. Feelings of intense emotion are not uncommon in the adolescent years, and they are a stage that many pass through. These feelings certainly do not make you a homosexual, though some may try to tell you they do.

But let's assume you are correct in preferring the same sex. What we have said makes it very clear that the Bible forbids sexual relations between men. So you either have to become celibate (have no sexual relationships at all) or change your orientation to a heterosexual one. No amount of wishing will make any difference to what God has clearly said. And that is also for your best good. There is no homosexual gene, despite what some research has tried to prove.

Homosexuality is an attitude and behaviour. Like other attitudes and behaviours it is learned. And as a result, like other behaviours it can be changed, and be turned back to God's original plan for human sexuality. Homosexuality is another part of 'broken sex' that includes other sins, and while offensive to many, should be treated as a sexual sin like others. In the biblical text, homosexuality is not identified as being worse than other forms of sexual transgression like immorality and adultery.

You ask what to do. Our best advice is to get some sympathetic counselling from a qualified individual and seek to understand yourself. Most of all, you need God's transforming power to be healed and remade in the image of God.

What is really wrong with being homosexual? I can't help the way I'm made.

A common argument that puts the blame on nature or on God. Homosexuality needs to be understood, not as a predetermined drive, but a learned sexual behaviour and attitude. Only by understanding God's reason for making male and female will there be an understanding of what is wrong in being a homosexual. But ultimately there is a choice, and to deny that choice is to deny God's power in your life.

Why is the Church so hard on homosexuals?

It shouldn't be. Like every other sin, the Church should love the sinner while hating the sin. Homosexuals are not to be excluded from salvation, but invited to come to a realization of their need to change and to accept God's healing salvation. Homophobia (fear and sometimes hatred of homosexuals) has no place in God's Church, which is a hospital for sinners, not a hotel for saints.

What is a sexual perversion?

Different people may give different answers. Our answer must be influenced by the Bible and by the teaching of Jesus. The Bible condemns homosexuality, bestiality, and sex with close relatives. The teaching of Jesus involves a loving respect for children and a reverence for the role of women. Hence sex with minors/children, and any form of sex that debases women must be regarded as perversion.

Why do you think adultery is so bad?

Look again at David and Bathsheba. Their lust did not only affect them, but it led to lies and deceit, the arranged murder of Bathsheba's husband, and a breakdown in respect for the monarchy (and God too). David and Bathsheba's actions, resulting in a damaged view of what was acceptable, had an impact throughout the country. For if the king can do it . . . . Adultery *always* has an impact, even if no one else knows about it. The broken self-esteem, the hidden guilt, the painful complicating of nearly every aspect of life — these are not considered in the heat of the moment, but they necessarily will and do come to haunt the adulterers. Most of all, adultery is a betrayal of trust, and a trust that reflects not only on your marriage partner, but on God too. For faith is trust in God, and if you break trust in any area of life, you compromise your trusting relationship to God. No wonder God used adultery as a picture to describe how He felt when betrayed by His children, Israel. Ultimately, *that's* why adultery is so bad.

Is it all right to get relief from looking at girlie magazines?

The suggestion is that your sexual drive is so desperate you *have* to get some relief. If that is so, then you obviously do not hold yourself in much esteem, otherwise you would not suggest you were totally under the control of your basic drives. Or perhaps this is just a good excuse. But are you aware of the dangers in

Devastation, broken self-esteem and guilt are the painful results of being rejected by your partner.

putting all these images into your mind, and feeding such sexual fantasies? No, we seriously answer that it is *not* all right.

11

SEX
the unhealthiest 'game'

But a man who commits adultery doesn't have any sense. He is just destroying himself. Proverbs 6:32.

JUST A GAME?

For some, sex is just a game they play. They get a buzz out of it. Every conquest is a challenge. Another name to add to their list.

But what they don't realize is that they're dicing with death. What kind of fun is it to gamble with your life?

For what the promoters of 'fun sex' don't tell you are all the problems it can bring. We've mentioned some of the emotional, mental and moral troubles. Now we need to mention the health hazards that sex can bring. Not to terrify you, but so that you can make a decision based on all the facts. And you owe it to yourself and your girl-friend to *know* the dangers that come with sex — in terms of some serious diseases. The truth is that sex can kill!

SO WHAT ARE THESE 'SEX DISEASES'?

Diseases which are mainly passed on through sexual activity are called STD (sexually-transmitted diseases) or VD (venereal diseases). Some are just unpleasant, others do serious damage, and then there are the diseases that can kill you. Many thousands of people around the world become infected every day. Don't believe it can't happen to you. It can!

GONORRHOEA

One of the most common sexually-transmitted diseases is gonorrhoea (or 'the clap'). This is caused by a bacterial infection. In many women there are no symptoms, but in men there's a discharge from the penis. Gonorrhoea can cause problems in urination, arthritis, and sterility (inability to have babies). If a pregnant woman is infected she will pass on her infection to her baby. The conjunctivae are affected. This, if left untreated, results in scarring and blindness. While antibiotics can cure this disease, some strains are becoming resistant to some drugs.

SYPHILIS

Syphilis was once a terrible curse that caused a great deal of pain and suffering. Long infection can cause damage to the heart, liver, kidneys, joints, brain and spinal cord. Modern drugs like penicillin were thought to spell the end for syphilis, but it is now increasing again and can be extremely dangerous if left untreated.

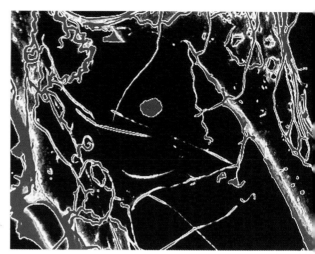

Syphilis (above) is an infectious venereal disease transmitted through sexual intercourse. If left untreated it can cause long-term damage to the blood supply, the nervous system, the skin, bones and brain. Gonorrhoea is also spread through intercourse and although not as devastating as syphilis has some serious effects in women on the urethra, vagina, cervix and in some cases the uterus and ovaries leading to sterility. It may also affect the rectum, mouth and eyes.

GENITAL WARTS

A virus is also responsible for genital warts. They are not painful, but are linked with an increased risk of cervical cancer. They can be removed by surgery. The presence of such warts on the genitals are of course a visible reminder of previous sexual activity.

THE HERPES VIRUSES

There are two Herpes viruses which cause infection. Type I causes facial and oral infection. Type II, genital herpes, is one of the commonest sexually-transmitted diseases and can cause much discomfort. It is usually noticed as blisters around the genitals which then turn into open sores. At the same time there may be fever, headache and swollen glands. Once infected, there may be outbreaks of this form of herpes later on. No cure has been found for this disease, caused by a virus. Some research indicates that herpes is linked to a higher risk of cancer of the cervix (in women).

CHLAMYDIA

Chlamydia is another bacterial infection which may only produce a burning sensation when urinating in men. In women it can cause serious pain and pregnancy problems. It can also make both men and women sterile.

Thrush, Trichomonas vaginalis and Gardnerella vaginalis are also sexually-transmitted diseases (more common in the West than syphilis). With these the male may not show symptoms or may have a urethritis.

AIDS

Acquired immune deficiency syndrome (AIDS) is the result of infection by the human immuno-deficiency virus (HIV) which destroys the body's defence against infections. The virus is passed on through bodily fluids, especially in semen, sexual secretions and blood. 'Safe sex' has been promoted as a way of avoiding AIDS, but the only safe way to avoid this infection is to avoid casual sex. Condoms do not provide complete protection, though they do reduce the risk. Though not everyone infected by the virus develops AIDS immediately, it is believed that everyone who is HIV positive will eventually develop AIDS. There is no cure for HIV infection or for AIDS.

Because of the great seriousness of the massive health threat posed by AIDS, we need to go into more detail here.

AIDS: THE ULTIMATE NIGHTMARE

The ongoing story of AIDS is a nightmare. And for those who suffer from AIDS, it is the ultimate nightmare. Because one out of one AIDS patients die. It might be nice to try to offer some pleasant words sug-gesting that a cure is just round the corner. But such words would be a lie.

AIDS was first reported in the late 70s in New York and San Francisco. By 1988 AIDS was recorded in 138 countries. By the end of the century, some forty million people are expected to have been infected with HIV, the virus that causes AIDS. Hundreds of thousands have already died from this dread disease, and many more will inevitably die.

ORIGIN AND SPREAD

The virus is similar to those found in chimpanzees and monkeys, and it is possible that this is where the virus originated. However, no one is certain as to where the virus came from, except that it appears to be a new human disease. AIDS has not been conclusively found in any samples before the 1970s. The virus is spread through body fluids, in particular semen and blood, from one person to another. The virus does not live long outside of the body, and so infection without direct contact with another person is unlikely.

So to be infected with HIV you need to have either had sex with an infected person, or have had a blood infusion with infected blood (or shared hypodermic needles — as some drug addicts do), or be the child of an infected mother (although not all children of an infected mother will be infected). Infection can occur after sex with a

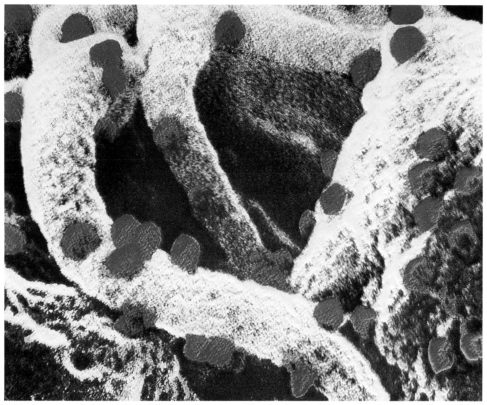

A highly enlarged view of the AIDS virus attacking white blood cells. This means that eventually the body loses its ability to fight infection.

man or a woman. The more sexual partners you have the more likely you are to become infected, though it is of course possible to be infected by just one other person.

The spread of HIV has been very fast in some groups at high risk. Homosexuals were the first such group to be recognized, along with intravenous drug users. However, the spread of the virus through the general population may also be rapid. In one African country, HIV infection in pregnant women attending a hospital was just 2 per cent in 1985. This rose to 19 per cent in 1988. Worse still, the figure rose to a massive 32 per cent in 1993. AIDS is the leading cause of death among young adults in a number of countries around the world.

HOW HIV WORKS

HIV works by damaging part of the body's defences against infection, so that other infections cannot be controlled. At first the body attacks the virus so it does not have a major effect for some time. It may not cause any major problems for

To be told by a doctor that you are infected by AIDS is a devastating blow. It means your life, sooner or later, will be cut short as a result of this modern 'plague'.

eight to ten years after infection. But then it develops into AIDS — when the defence system breaks down and all kinds of diseases are able to take hold. The virus is amazingly productive — up to a thousand million a day — and once the body's defences are broken, the progression of AIDS can be very rapid.

The infections which may enter through this 'open door' include an unusual form of pneumonia, various stomach infections, cancers of the lymph glands, skin diseases, and a formerly rare kind of cancer called Kaposi's sarcoma. Along with a general tiredness and sickness, weight loss and diarrhoea, AIDS has a ter-rible catalogue of possible diseases. Because the disease works by making you defenceless against even such 'bugs' that cause an upset stomach in healthy people, it can be a painful and lingering death.

HOW YOU CAN AVOID AIDS

The only sure way is not to have sex with an infected person (leaving aside the other ways of being infected — like through blood, or being the child of an infected mother). And since you can't tell by looking who is infected and who isn't, then to have sex with anyone is to take a severe risk. Condoms do protect to some extent, but even so one in five using condoms are still infected by sex with someone with the virus.

The AIDS test is not totally reliable (there are both false positives and false negatives), and in any case may not detect the virus in the first few months. So even if someone says they have had a test and it was OK doesn't guarantee they don't have the virus.

Since there is no treatment to cure AIDS and no way to make sex totally 'safe', you will be wise to avoid sex altogether outside of marriage. Within a marriage, with both partners faithful, there is no chance of getting AIDS, unless one was infected by having sex before marriage.

THE NIGHTMARE

The nightmare is not only for

those who have become infected, but those they love and care for, and the whole of society. What of the regret of admitting to your fiancée you are HIV positive? What of your relationships with your family? What of the children you would like to have? Will they become infected too? Will you live to see them grow up? Will they thank you for your foolish actions?

And what of those who are infected without acting foolishly? The wives who acquire the virus from their husbands? The women who are raped? The little girls who are sexually abused, even by family members?

We all pay a great price for the evil actions of others. Whole villages destroyed by AIDS, families torn apart, children orphaned and doomed to die themselves.

The ultimate nightmare is with us.

Research into HIV has been extensive and expensive. Now and again the media reports possible cures but an effective remedy seems as elusive as ever. Prevention is still the essential element in combating this killer disease.

So what is *your* choice?

See also the feature: THE UN-SEEN KILLER on page 158.

MAKING DECISIONS

After reading all the horrible aspects of sexually-transmitted diseases, you can become very fearful and anxious. You may even convince yourself that you have one of these diseases. Like students studying to become doctors think they have every disease they read about, it's not normally true.

But if you have a reason to believe you have been infected by having sex with someone and have some symptoms like sores around the genitals, with headaches, sweats or fever — then it would be good to be checked by a doctor. While it may be embarrassing, it is very dangerous not to have treatment. Genito-urinary medicine clinics — 'Special Clinics' — have been set up in many countries. They are walk-in clinics for those who are too embarrassed to consult their family physician.

All these possible diseases are a good reason to think seriously about the question, 'Why wait?' Waiting for sex in marriage with a partner who is (and has been) faithful means you have nothing to worry about.

More than that, the fewer sexual partners you and your girl-friend or wife have had reduces the risk. So if you have had sex before marriage, it's no reason to go on doing it. You are less likely to be infected if you have not had sex with many girls.

All this talk about infections may also mean that you will have some difficult talks with your girl-friend. You owe it to each other to be honest. For if either of you is infected, then that particular disease can be passed on to the other. Love must be honest, and would you wish to put her at risk? And would you wish to become infected by any of these diseases? For if something is discovered later, it can destroy a marriage. Marriage is based on honesty and trust. You need to be honest and trusting beforehand too.

OTHER ASPECTS OF SEX

Perhaps the most obvious possible consequence — and yet frequently forgotten or ignored — is conception: the making of a baby! Pregnancy is as much the boy's trauma as the girl's (or should be!). So contraception is as much the boy's responsibility as the girl's. All too often what should be a wonderful event is turned into a tragedy. The results of that can be truly life-changing, and sadly for the worse. The girl has to make some very difficult decisions, and life will never be quite the same again. Supportive parents and friends can be a big help, and the modern rush to 'take care of it' through abortion has to be avoided.

The whole subject of abortion is very wide and emotive. However, it is our conviction both from experience and belief, that abortion simply

Babies are always a possible consequence of sex — a wonderful climax to a secure marriage — but in a relationship outside of marriage they are not often welcome.

to destroy an unwanted pregnancy is very wrong. Aside from all the ethical arguments over the sanctity of life, the woman cannot help but experience loss and guilt — feelings which may last a very long time. Those relatively rare situations of having to choose between the life of the mother or the baby, life-threatening genetic disorders, rape, incest and so on are matters of conscience that have to be decided individually. The general situation of abortion because of convenience is to be resisted.

Of those who have had abortions of convenience we have counselled, most have expressed their deep feelings of regret. Decisions taken quickly, and sometimes under duress, are not infrequently seen as being great mistakes.

Every act of sexual intercourse must be seen as a possibility to conceive. So you must ask yourself, 'Am I ready for fatherhood? Have I the right to force motherhood on an immature girl? Who would look after the baby? My parents? Her parents?' What about the rights of the child to enjoy love and security? Parenthood is a heavy responsibility and should not be entered into without care and thought.

CONTRACEPTION

Often contraception is suggested as the cure-all for such concerns. The line is: 'If you've taken precautions, then go ahead and enjoy yourself.'

What's wrong with that advice?

☐ Contraception is never 100 per cent foolproof. Contraceptive pills are safe enough; but only if the woman always remembers to take them. And if you're not really planning to have a sexual relationship, would she have pills handy if you were carried away by the 'passion of the moment'? Condoms are certainly not totally effective, especially in inexperienced hands. Other methods such as IUDs and diaphragms for the woman again are not completely reliable, and require a degree of premeditation (you both decide: we're getting ready for sex).

☐ Condoms provide some protection from the diseases mentioned above, but not total protection. Other forms of contraception do not protect you from infection. Those same risks still apply.

☐ What about those 'mental health' consequences? How will you feel? What about guilt and the loss of self-esteem? Just because you've taken precautions against conceiving, should you really be sexually active? Is this experience really going to be good for you?

☐ What will this do to your relationship? Sex, as we have seen, can be very destructive — and all too often is not the cement of a relationship but the dynamite that blows it apart. Secret sex in shabby surroundings — is that what you both really want?

MENTAL CONSEQUENCES

Parallel to the physical consequences of sex are the mental and emotional consequences — and may be even more significant sometimes. The disharmony of giving yourself fully when you cannot honestly make such a commitment, the living of a lie in what is really happening in your life, the sense of shame or remorse or low self-esteem can lead to further problems.

The problem of guilt is perhaps the most terrible of consequences. Some modern therapists have tried to deal with guilt through denial. 'You have no need to feel guilty, it's OK', or so they say. Trouble is, this way of thinking often leads to further problems. For if you can deny your guilt you may end up thinking nothing is wrong, or alternatively your denial of guilt will compound the sense of wrong and make it worse. Whatever the case, guilt cannot be dealt with by saying it's not there. Guilt craves healing and forgiveness, and to tell someone who believes they are wrong that they are not is surely an even greater wrong!

Damage to your mental health through wrong, perverted or mis-

Guilt is a stubborn companion and refuses to go away even when the problem is resolved. It is hard to forgive yourself and memory has the habit of reminding you of your bad experiences.

guided sex is very real. Sleeplessness, anxiety attacks, general lassitude, trouble concentrating, forgetfulness, headaches — all may have their origins in concerns over sex. Because sex by definition is supposed to involve another, relationships are very much affected. In sexual wrong there is no 'victimless crime'. For not only are you a victim of your own mistakes, but others are too — innocent or not.

One teenage girl came to see us and eventually admitted to a long-standing sexual relationship with a married man. They both realized

Allowing your life to be obsessed with sex may mean you find difficulty in concentrating on matters which are crucial to your future.

their affair was wrong, and had often tried to end it. But the physical desire had always proved too strong, whatever their mental decisions. Now they had both become very depressed, and had low self-esteem, particularly due to their inability to end the relationship.

'Confessing' (admitting to a third party) the problem was the first step in preventing and healing the relationship. No longer was it 'their little secret'. Step by step the separation was achieved, gradually making them less dependent upon each other, forcing them to turn their interests elsewhere. And after many months it was safe to say the affair was over, and the rebuilding of their separate selves was beginning. The emotional scars of any such relationship take a long while healing — and yet in order to have some self-respect, this is an essential process.

Wrong sex has its physical dangers which can be identified and measured. But the damage to human lives, feelings and personalities is incalculable, and affects the whole stability of human life, meaning and purpose.

PREVENTION

Prevention is so much better than cure. To make your own decisions rather than allow others to make them for you will increase your self-respect and self-confidence. Just because others are foolish, you don't have to go along with the crowd. The information in this chapter is

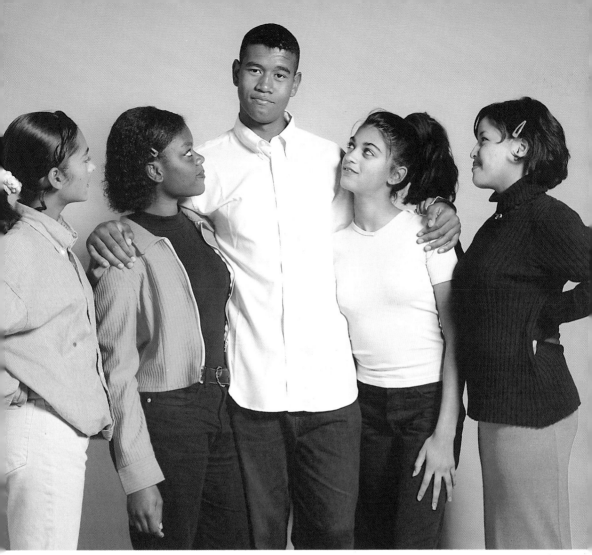

When the emotional pressure is on and somehow your principles don't seem quite such high priority, remember you are in charge of your lifestyle.

designed to help you choose, giving you evidence on which to base your choice.

OK, sometimes it's not easy to make logical decisions in the middle of a passionate kiss! So make your decisions beforehand, and stick to them — in that way you'll stay right and also keep your self-esteem.

CONCLUSION

What all this shows is that sex is too powerful and too dangerous to be let loose in a 'free-for-all'. Sex needs to be channelled with love, in a relationship of trust and knowledge. When, as husband and wife, you are sure that you can relax in each others' arms, having confidence that no cross-infecting will occur, maybe practising contraception but not too worried if your wife does conceive, mentally confident and without guilt or shame — then sex can be brilliant. Otherwise, it will always be less than perfect, defective merchandise that will leave you disappointed instead of truly satisfied.

AIDS: THE UNSEEN KILLER

Imagine. If you were to make up some story about some invisible yet deadly contamination that was spread through the most intimate form of love, it would be seen as madness or some kind of sick joke. Just a few years ago such a scenario would have appeared absurd. But not today.

The reality of AIDS is just that — the unseen killer that enters the body to do its deadly work. It is spread most commonly today by sexual intercourse. This nightmare has become a chilling reality around the world, with some societies being wiped out by this modern plague. The statistics hardly express the horror: worldwide it is estimated HIV infects about 15 million people, with a projected 40-50 million within the next five years. And as time continues it seems likely that just about every one of these people infected with the HIV virus will eventually develop AIDS.

Add to this all the extra suffering when children are orphaned and families broken apart and you have a massive crisis that is beyond belief. The more so because what hope can be offered to the AIDS sufferer? The infections associated with the body's reduced immune ability can be treated. But it is a one way street, as the virus slowly but surely cripples the defence mechanisms. Those hoping for some vaccine or other will be disappointed for a long while, say the researchers, since the virus

mutates (changes) so often it cannot be 'pinned down'. In fact it is this ability to change its 'appearance' to the body so often which is the reason why the normal way the body takes care of such invaders doesn't work.

So what exactly is this HIV virus? A virus is a tiny 'particle' of life that can only exist as a kind of parasite inside another living being. You can only see a virus by using a very powerful microscope. There are many other viruses like herpes and the common cold. They work by using the living materials around them to develop and grow, and then spread into other parts of their host. The HIV virus is a kind of 'germ' that the body does not recognize very well as being dangerous, and which attacks the system that protects against other kinds of infection and disease.

So you could say that AIDS doesn't kill anyone. What it does is to make you so vulnerable to common diseases that they can kill you. These 'opportunist' invaders take over the weakened body, leading eventually to death from such complications.

The virus attacks in particular the immune system, the bowel, skin and brain. The skin may itch and may develop cancers that are usually rarely found. The brain may become affected and dementia results. Infection of the bowel is shown in severe diarrhoea accompanied by dramatic weight loss. And so on. The end results are appalling.

But at first the infection is generally

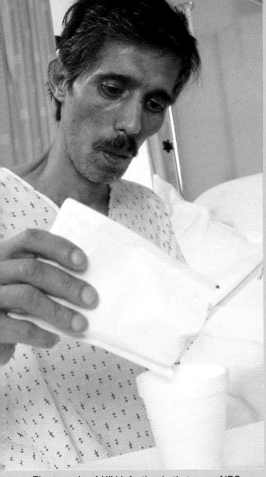

The tragedy of HIV infection is that once AIDS develops there is no way out, it leaves orphans and broken families.

unnoticed. The virus may not produce any symptoms for between five and twelve years. Most do not know they are infected until the virus has done great damage to the immune system.

So, knowing the hard facts, what should be our reaction? Firstly one of compassion and support for those who are suffering from AIDS. Those who call this a plague from God ignore all those who are suffering without choice. And what of those who have acted wrongly in sexual matters and have *not* become infected? Is that to be seen as the blessing of God upon what He has identified as sexual immorality?

Then must come understanding of how the virus is passed on. To want to avoid infectious people is understandable. But the evidence is that normal contact does not pose any material risk. The virus is passed on by four main ways. Sexual intercourse (homo- and hetero-sexual), intravenous drug use (shared needles), transfusions of infected blood and the use of infected blood products, and to the children of an infected mother. Other examples such as infected dentists passing on the virus to their patients are significant because of their rarity.

This, in turn, must lead everyone to ask what they should do. 'Safe sex' is a common term today, but it should be remembered that sex with a partner infected with HIV can never be made totally safe. Condoms reduce the risk, but only down to about 20 per cent of the risk if you did not use a condom. That is still a risk that most would not be happy to gamble with. The reason that condoms are recommended is because they provide some protection, and slow down the spread of the virus. But what if you happen to be one of the 20 per cent?

A few myths also need to be exploded. You cannot become infected by HIV 'through the air' as you might expect to catch a cold. You cannot catch it from touch, sharing a cup or using a public toilet. You cannot be infected just by the variety of sexual activities you and your partner perform, so long as neither of you has had sex with anyone else. (We know of one woman who was worried that a specific sexual act would give her AIDS, even though she was sure

It is well known that the syringe-swapping junkie and the homosexual are at the greatest risk from AIDS but so are promiscuous heterosexuals.

her husband was faithful to her.) Nor is AIDS the punishment for premarital sex as someone once told us, even though he was aware that both he and his partner were both virgins.

Unless you are one of the other three groups mentioned above (someone infected through blood transfusion, a drug abuser who shared needles, or the child of an infected mother), the *only* route of any significance is sexual intercourse. If ever there was a good reason to avoid sex and wait until marriage with someone you know and trust, it's now!

'I don't believe it will happen to me,' some say. But the statistics say differently. And you cannot decide that he or she 'looks' clean. HIV infection is nothing to do with cleanliness or hygiene. There is no such visible test for HIV. And even the medical professionals admit that there is a 'window' during which someone who has become infected can still show negative when tested — maybe even up to twelve months later. So even a certificate from the doctor is no guarantee.

And because of the fear of AIDS, many refuse to go and take a test, or pretend nothing is really wrong because they don't want to know. As a result, the virus spreads through ignorance, fear and indifference.

So if we cannot look to a cure, if we cannot make 'safe sex' safe, then only by following celibacy (no sex) or marriage (with no premarital or extra-marital sex) can there be true security.

AIDS is a threat too dangerous and

too common to be ignored. Do you, your partner, and your children have to become part of those terrible statistics? You make the choice, no one else.

So far we've just looked at the medical impact of AIDS, along with its effect on whole societies. But there is a deeper kind of impact, an ever more damaging kind of loss.

Perhaps the worst of all is a kind of self-disgrace. How you have failed yourself, and thrown your life away — or at least condemned yourself to a future of pain and regret. Then there's the loss of friends, as few can handle the emotional burden that AIDS brings in its wake. And what of the Church which, though it should be caring, has members for whom AIDS is a terrible fear? And what if there is an unchristian life-style? Can you still be a member? Or what of trust and confidence in marriage, now or in the future? And those repeated spiritual questions: 'Why me? Is God to blame? Couldn't He have prevented it? Or is He cursing me too?'

The unseen killer strikes, and because there is no cure, you may live for some while — but the death sentence is already passed. Though some are able to make their years fulfilling, and find comfort and consolation and a sense of worth — the tragedy is still there.

So what will you choose?

There are no visible tests for HIV infection. Only a blood-test can provide the information which could tell you if you are infected.

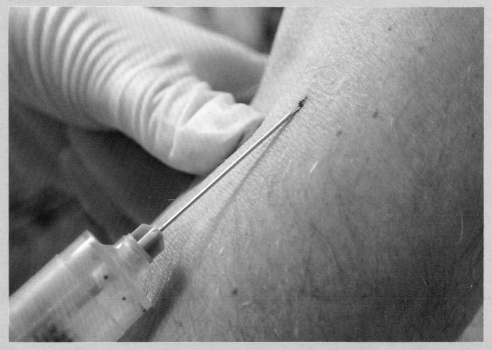

QUESTIONS AND ANSWERS

I think I have caught something from a girl I slept with. I'm so embarrassed and feel absolutely terrible. What should I do?

Go and see a doctor — now; either your family doctor or a doctor at one of the Special Clinics. Do all you're told. Tell the girl. She needs to get treatment too. Don't sleep around any more. But most of all remember that God still loves you, and forgives you if you ask. You haven't committed the unpardonable sin. But don't ignore the problem. You need to sort yourself out, both physically and spiritually. Take this as a health warning about your life-style — and change!

How should the Church view AIDS?

Some have identified AIDS as a curse from God. If that were absolutely true, then God would be cursing haemophiliacs (people needing blood products because of a hereditary disease), unborn children, innocent partners and so on. Even those dealing in illegal drugs who catch AIDS from shared needles may be foolish, but they are not necessarily evil. And just because someone commits some sexual sin, should the punishment be death? Has God suddenly changed the rules? No: we must see AIDS as being linked to this sinful world, and the innocent suffer along with the guilty. It remains true that if everyone had been faithful in marriage, and had no sex before marriage,

there would be no AIDS epidemic. But like all sin, the Church condemns the sin and not the sinner.

Are condoms effective in preventing sexually-transmitted diseases?

They help. But there's no such thing as safe sex — except not to do it. Some statistics suggest that even when condoms are used, they are only 80 per cent effective in preventing the spread of STDs. *That means a failure rate of about one in five* — far too high to feel safe. Obviously if you are going to have sex, then condoms should be used with the intention of preventing disease and pregnancy. But you must be aware that this still carries risks, and doesn't protect against mental and spiritual difficulties.

Wouldn't it be better to be prepared for sex by using contraceptives than not to think about them at all?

Christians have a problem here. For if you're thinking about having sex, and so decide to get hold of contraceptives beforehand, you're 'planning to sin' as one young person put it. If you don't plan, then your girl-friend may get pregnant (or catch a disease). That's why its statistically more likely that Christian girls become pregnant — because they are not intending to have unprotected sex. The only way is to make your decisions beforehand. You are either going to be true to Christian principles, and not have sexual intercourse; or you are going to and so take precautions. You cannot be in two minds about this.

I heard that most venereal diseases are easily cured, so they don't really matter today. Is this true?

No. Though syphilis has been well controlled by drugs, and gonorrhoea too, both have been increasing, especially gonorrhoea which in some cases has become resistant to some drugs. Syphilis can take a long time to diagnose and this can lead to permanent damage. While medical advances have helped in treatment, they haven't been able to stop a great increase in the spread of sexually-transmitted diseases. They are still dangerous, and of course AIDS has no cure at the moment. Don't be fooled; they can do much damage and you take real risks in having sex, especially on a casual basis.

I have felt so worthless and guilty after having sex. It was nothing like I expected, and now I feel as if I've messed up my whole life. God must think I'm really bad, and I don't like myself for what I've done.

In many ways, these words express the most damaging side of sexual health problems. Although the physical diseases are a terrible threat, to feel useless and worthless means your whole life seems to be wasted. We don't know your situation, but we do know that God doesn't give up on anyone who wants help and healing. You need to see yourself as being of special value

Never persuade yourself that you are worthless. God will never give up on you whatever you have done. To Him you are very special.

to God. You are unique — there's no one like you in the whole wide world. You are special — that's why God came to this world, to save you, you personally. And who are you to see yourself as nothing if God says you're special? Read the last two chapters and see how God can make a way back to a worthwhile life, free from guilt and spiritual pain.

12

Ending guilt, becoming free

Freedom is what we have — Christ has set us free! Stand, then, as free people, and do not allow yourselves to become slaves again. Galatians 5:1.

SEXUAL FREEDOM AND RESPONSIBILITY

Are we free sexually? Like any other area, as Christians, we can answer with an emphatic 'Yes!' Does this mean then we can do anything sexual, use our bodies in any way? Emphatically not! For as Paul also makes clear, 'Should we continue to live in sin so that God's grace will increase? Certainly not!' (Romans 6:1, 2.) For if we follow our sinful lusts, then, 'What human nature does is quite plain. It shows itself in immoral, filthy, and indecent actions.' (Galatians 5:19.)

What Christ has done is to set us free to choose. Christ sets us free through His law of liberty (James 1:25; 2:12) from the bondage of sin: our sinful desires, our evil habits, our wrong thoughts and actions. And 'where the Spirit of the Lord is present, there is freedom.' (2 Corinthians 3:17.) This is not sexual licence to sin — far from it. On the contrary, it is the freedom to choose

to use God's gift of sexuality in the right way.

Instead of being slaves to our sexual lusts, we can live truly and honestly, controlling our sexuality and making sure its expression is the very best, as God intended. 'For the law of the Spirit, which brings life in union with Christ Jesus, has set me free from the law of sin and death.' (Romans 8:2.) The slavery of sexual desire leads only to sin and death — to a meaningless series of physical sensations without any spiritual element. God sets us free from this compulsion. We are no longer dominated by our physical drives; rather we control them. Instead of being 'sexual robots' we can use our controlled sexuality to good benefit. We think of others before our own satisfaction.

Not only are we set free from sexual compulsion, we are also set free from sexual guilt. If Christ's message means anything at all, it is forgiveness and healing for the guilt-damaged sinner. Guilt is helpful in bringing us back to God, but we must leave our guilt there and not try to keep on carrying it once we know we have asked for and have received God's forgiveness. Since sexual sin and the resulting guilt is so intensely personal, this can be so difficult. But just *because* it is so close to us means that accepting freedom from guilt is that much more important. If you have sexual guilt, have asked for and received God's forgiveness, then apply this to any guilt feeling that may remain: 'There is no condemnation now for those who live in union with Christ Jesus.' (Romans 8:1.)

God's freedom is also liberty from this world's sexual concepts and laws. While some rules follow divine principles, others do not. The unnecessary suffering caused through wrong sexual beliefs needs to be healed. For example, old wives' tales about the physical dangers of sexual activities (masturbation, different positions, oral sex, etc.) have led to some great mental harm and associated burdens of guilt. Where God has not legislated, we should not either.

The basic principle of loving unselfishness must be the foundation of all Christian sexual ethics, not the austere regulations of authority figures that may themselves have sexual phobias. Once again, let us repeat that this is not to say that the Christian can do as he pleases. 'The body is not to be used for sexual immorality, but to serve the Lord.' (1 Corinthians 6:13.) Rather God's freedom points out that social ideas of sexuality and its expression do not necessarily match biblical principles and the divine ideal.

For ultimately the freedom of God is freedom from the false concepts of sexuality that plague this modern world. The impression is given in sex manuals that providing you have developed your sexual technique then life will be totally meaningful and problem free. While sexual skills are important for the mutual pleasure of husband and wife, they do not in themselves bring the abundant life of which Jesus spoke. You may be an amazing sexual athlete, but still be empty and unfulfilled. Orgasm is no substitute for the glorious experience of knowing God and His salvation!

God frees us from the illusions of sex that we have painted on the walls of our minds, and allows us to experience sexuality in its deeper and more spiritual aspects as we commit ourselves in unselfish love to one woman, and not a succession of genital encounters.

Instead of the delusion of spiritual substitutes through 'the joy of sex' (casual, incomplete, only physical), we find true happiness through the right use our sexuality. We discover the true joy of sex by limiting our sexual expression to one person at the right time and place in Christian marriage. And amazingly, by limiting ourselves in this way our freedom is extended — to explore our sexuality more deeply and more intensely than we could ever think possible!

REPENTANCE

But before we take God's freedom as a licence to follow our own sinful ways, remember that Jesus did not tell those who refused to repent that they were forgiven. Forgiveness comes with the clear understanding that there is a sincere desire to change, a repentance for past evil. Added to God's forgiveness of us is the vital need for us to forgive others:

'"If you forgive others the wrongs they have done to you, your Father in heaven will also forgive you. But if you will not forgive others, then your Father will not forgive the wrongs you have done."' (Matthew 6:14, 15.)

The message Jesus preached was, '"Turn away from your sins, because the Kingdom of heaven is near!"' (Matthew 4:17.) In His charge to His disciples in Luke Jesus made it clear that '"in his name the message about repentance and the forgiveness of sins must be preached to all nations."' (Luke 24:47.) Nowhere in Jesus' teaching is there any hint of cheap grace, of saying that sin is not sin, that it doesn't matter what you do. But to those willing to acknowledge their sins He was ready and happy to offer forgiveness and peace.

As God had told His people cen-

Many teenagers feeling devalued and rejected have turned to alcohol for relief, only to find guilt and their problems haven't gone away.

turies before: 'I have set before you life and death, blessings and curses. Now choose life, so that you and your children may live and that you may love the Lord your God . . . .' (Deuteronomy 30:19, NIV.) His desperate appeal is 'Choose life', knowing that if they did not give up their wicked ways, then He would be forced to give them up, as in the end He had to (see Romans 1:21, 24, 28).

Repentance comes as a result of realizing how wrong we are. Only when we acknowledge we are sinful can the process begin — by going to God and wanting to be changed.

HOW TO DEAL WITH SEXUAL GUILT

The first step is to admit the situation and the guilt. All too often problems are related to denial — that is to refuse to admit the problem! Even here there are complications — for what some may be guilty about may not be a serious sexual sin, while for others with hardened consciences sin may not be seen as sin at all.

Next step is to want to do something about it. That may seem an obvious statement, but all too many identify their guilt but not wish to change the situation — believing perhaps that they will 'lose their love' or some similar idea. We have to realize that actions have consequences, and doing nothing about sexual sin will also have damaging consequences for us too.

Third step is actively to seek forgiveness and change. This may be done through a counsellor, or directly with God. We need to see God not as hostile and threatening, but willing to hear and respond to our sinful state through His loving forgiveness.

The fourth step is to accept God's forgiveness. Often this is the hardest aspect — for our guilt may appear so overwhelming we cannot believe that it can be easily forgiven. In the words of Alfred Korzybski: 'God may forgive your sins but your nervous system won't.' We know of Christians who have asked for forgiveness time and time again, and yet still maintain they do not 'feel' forgiven.

And it is this concentration on 'feeling' that is at the problem of dealing with guilt. Thoughts of shame and humiliation cloud judgement, and make sexual sin harder to deal with than many others. This does not mean that sexual sin is any worse than other sins, but because it is so close to home, so intimately involved with who we truly *are*, then to be objective about sin and forgiveness is honestly impossible.

For this reason we must trust God and take Him at His word:

'As far as the east is from the west, so far has he removed our transgressions from us.' Psalm 103:12, NIV.

'You will tread our sins underfoot and hurl our iniquities into the depths of the sea.' Micah 7:19, NIV.

'"Though your sins are like scarlet, they shall be white as snow."' Isaiah 1:18, NIV.

'"I will forgive their wickedness and will remember their sins no more."' Jeremiah 31:34, NIV.

That's what God says to us, each one of us. And we can all identify with that wonderful confession of David's repentance and God's forgiveness in Psalm 51.

And what of '"Forgive, and you will be forgiven"' (Luke 6:37, NIV)? This text also includes ourselves, for as we believe ourselves to have been forgiven, *and forgive ourselves*, then we will believe we are truly forgiven.

God's forgiveness is not just the legal way He takes care of sin. More

than forgiveness *for* sin, God wants to reclaim us *from* sin. We are not to see God as being concerned to take care of the 'sin account' but rather that we are rescued from our own perverted desires that lead us into sin in the first place. Otherwise God's forgiveness would simply be some kind of mechanical device to 'fix you up again' every time you sinned — like a repeated cleaning-up operation which lasts only as long as the time it takes to get dirty again!

To see forgiveness as simply taking care of your legal problem can lead to some terrible misunderstandings. You may come to believe that as long as you've remembered to ask forgiveness for every sin, then you're OK. You want to make sure you've taken care of business, and you worry that there might be one 'unconfessed sin' you could have forgotten about. And you're anxious that should you die without having the chance to ask forgiveness, you won't be saved.

On the other hand, some don't worry about sin because they believe God is always there to take care of it. If you sin, well never mind, because God will forgive. As one French philosopher put it, 'It's His business.' So just take it for granted, and don't worry about what you do.

Both these ideas are wrong because they see forgiveness only in terms of taking care of some legal charge that is made against the sinner. They fail to take into account the *effects* of sin, and the deep-seated causes of sin in our lives.

When one young man visited us he was in total despair. He felt he had completely ruined his life, and that of his girl-friend, and others in his family. We don't need to go into all his story, but he had certainly done some awful things. He had even gone so far as to contemplate suicide, believing he had done so much wrong that there was no way back.

But as we explained to him, there is never a situation that God cannot handle. That's not to say you don't have to live with some dreadful consequences. But whatever you have done, you have not committed the unpardonable sin. How can we be so sure? Because the unpardonable sin is the one for which you don't *want* to be forgiven. If you are convinced of your sin, and want forgiveness, then that is proof that the Spirit is still working with you.

You may believe that you have committed some terrible sins. You may be overcome with guilt and remorse. You may even feel you have totally destroyed your relationship with God and that you can never come back to Him.

But the truth is that God never turns anyone away. The Devil would like you to believe that there's no hope for you, that you have sinned away any possibility of forgiveness.

Healing is a process that only comes as you share your problems, as you acknowledge your helpless condition, and as you find forgiveness from the injured and from God.

Unthinking presents, careless words, thoughtless even selfish decisions especially about money can affect relationships but 'love keeps no record of wrongs' is an essential principle that heals and keeps people together.

But the worse you are, and the worse you feel as a result, the more you need the God of healing forgiveness!

Remember when Peter asked Jesus how many times he should forgive — and felt pretty pious in suggesting seven times. It was the God of forgiveness who showed His true character in Jesus' answer of 'seventy times seven'.

'Love keeps no record of wrongs' (1 Cor. 13:5, NIV); and God is not working on our bad-good balance sheet! What He wants to do is to release us from our chains of guilt and shame, to make us whole

IF YOU'VE BEEN HURT

(All these comments are general because we do not know your situation. But they can apply to all kinds of hurts and wrongs that you may have experienced.)

DON'T IGNORE IT

You need to deal with the situation. To let it fester inside you can be the worst thing to do. And if you have been abused or physically hurt that means not just asking God to forgive the one who did this, but going and doing something about it. For it may not only be you, but others — in the past, and in the future too — unless you take steps to have the guilty person exposed.

SPEAK TO SOMEONE YOU TRUST

Talk to God, of course, asking for His help in working through all the negative emotions. But talk to trustworthy Christians too. The Bible demonstrates the way in which other believers were able to help those in trouble. This is the way God works — through His followers and the gifts that God gives to each.

LOOK TO GOD FOR HEALING

Healing from pain, anger and bitterness. For if you hold on to these feelings then you will never move past the present. Don't allow whatever wrong was done to you to do more damage through resentment and hatred.

MOVE FORWARD

We are people of hope, and that hope is the renewing process that God does in the present. We leave the past behind us, and press forward towards the mark — the calling of God to an eternal future with Him.

once more. In the words of Dag Hammarskjöld: 'Forgiveness is the answer to the child's dream of a miracle by which what is broken is made whole again, what is soiled is again made clean.'

We must not fool ourselves, though. As we are, we are lost, broken, fatally sin-sick. We cannot say forgiveness does not matter, or it is not important. Nor can we say that we are basically good and just need some 'cosmetic surgery' to make us look great in God's sight. Jesus speaks about a total life-change — that we all need to be born again.

And if you should think this must happen overnight, look again at the lives of other Christians, and realize how long God has worked with them. Look at self-confident Peter, at arrogant Paul. Look at the list of the heroes (and heroines) of faith in Hebrews 11. Think of Rahab, the prostitute, and that she is included in this list of the faithful. And as we are particularly concerned with sexual sin and its healing, what of Mary Magdalene too?

SO HOW?

What is needed is a how to — how to lose the heavy baggage of our sinful actions and their results in our lives. We have found words like the following helpful to those suffering from the pain of sexual guilt. We suggest you think deeply about what they are saying to you personally. They are our message to you:

'What you need is peace — not of this world, but the peace of Heaven. You are desperate for that rest and quiet deep inside, but nothing you have tried brings what you want. Money can't buy such peace, nor can your career or your qualifications or your achievements or your ambitions or your search for pleasure. Your sins seem to be always before you, condemning you and turning your life into a war zone. But God wants to give you such peace as His own special gift. That is His promise to you — to take away the pain and hurt and guilt, and make you whole again. More than that God wants to make you in His image — to be like Him! As you come to God admitting your sinfulness and wanting to repent, He comes close beside you with mercy and sympathy and forgiveness.

'Don't make the mistake of believing you have to make yourself right first. The idea that you have to achieve some level of goodness before you can come to God is totally wrong. Why? First it stops you coming to God, and second you can't make yourself good anyway.

'Come to Christ just as you are, and think about His love until your hard and sin-soaked heart is broken. Remember David, who came to God

Sin separates and brings bad feelings of disappointment, rejection, broken dreams and alienation. But, all is not lost, reconciliation, renewal and healing are possible because God longs to help.

after committing adultery with Bathsheba, saying: "A broken and contrite heart, O God, you will not despise." (Psalm 51:17, NIV). Realize the love that God has shown you, even though you're not worthy of it. Realize that God has broken every barrier down. Realize that nothing needs to prevent you from accepting God's offer of merciful forgiveness. Because even your desire to repent comes from God. There is nothing to pay, no penance to make, nothing in you that is of any worth to buy forgiveness. Only the gracious gift of God, who loves you as His very special son. So come home, and be reconciled to God!'

What does that mean for the way we live, and how we treat one another? We need to remember that we do not receive forgiveness *because* we forgive but *as* we forgive. The source of all forgiveness is that, 'While we were yet sinners, Christ died for us.' (Romans 5:8.) As a result we should, 'Be kind and compassionate to one another, forgiving each other, just as in Christ God forgave you.' (Ephesians 4:32, NIV.)

Although it doesn't come in gift wrap, God's love *is* a gift, you don't have to earn it, you don't have to be good, all you have to do is accept it.

QUESTIONS AND ANSWERS

What if I don't really agree that what the Bible says is a sin is wrong?

To him who believes it is a sin, then it is. And even though you say you disagree with the Bible, it's hard to argue with the results. We imagine you're thinking about what the Bible calls sexual sin, rather than believing it's OK to murder or steal or something. Just because modern society has different values (or even no values at all!) doesn't mean that what the Bible says is wrong. Just take a look at what happens when you go against Christian sexual principles. Isn't it likely you're only trying to justify yourself, or trying to ease your conscience?

I've tried to be good, but I keep on falling. I'm feeling like there's no hope for me, and that I'll never make it. Help!

God never gives up — not until you finally walk away from Him. So don't listen to the whispers of the Devil on how many times you've sinned and how you can't be forgiven. It's not true. We all fail in many ways, and yet God still patiently helps us up to continue. Never believe there's no hope, for God is the God of Hope. And if you allow Him, He will re-make you in His image, and you will be right with Him once more.

Sometimes I feel I haven't really lived. I grew up in the Church and haven't

done many bad things, especially not with sex. I wonder about all the things people confess about, and wish I had something more to say too. Do you think this is right?

No! You need to understand all the pain and hurt and damage that comes from living apart from God's way. You should count your blessings and be glad that you've been spared so much by having Christian principles to start with. Don't be worried you haven't got anything to 'confess' to, instead thank God for the opportunity to show how good it is not to get mixed up in 'broken sex' in the first place!

I have done some things — sexual things — that I'm really ashamed about. I don't think I can ever forgive myself. What should I do?

One word: repent. And accept the forgiveness that only God can give, the peace that passes all understanding (see Philippians 4:7). And if God can forgive you, can you be so arrogant to say you can't forgive yourself? Do all you can to make the wrong things right, and thank God for His all-changing grace that makes you into his trustworthy son once more.

I love my girl-friend but we don't seem to get on, especially physically. Sometimes I feel that even when things are good they're bad, and I get really

goals, maybe you're not planning to stay together anyway. Perhaps you've had a heavy sexual relationship that no longer seems right; or is it that what you thought would be wonderful no longer satisfies? Like a sign we saw on the side of a church, 'If God seems a long way away, who moved?' It wasn't God, and if your current relationship and way of life have taken you away from God then it cannot be good for you. Take time to rediscover God, experience His healing forgiveness, and decide what you really want in life!

I know God has forgiven me for having sex without being married. But how do I forgive myself?

One of the hardest questions — because we may almost *want* to suffer as a way of feeling we're being punished for doing wrong. Also involved is the whole concept of self-perception — how do I see myself? Do you tell yourself: 'I'm pathetic, I've made a mess of things . . . ', and then go on to remind yourself of everything evil and sinful? Unless you can catch a glimpse of being someone better, of understanding that God sees great potential in you, it *will* be hard to forgive yourself. But until you do, you can't move forward. And to say that you can't forgive yourself, even though God can, is being rather arrogant, isn't it? We need to be careful that we don't throw God's healing forgiveness back in His face. See yourself for what you are, certainly, but then see what you (with God) can be. And don't wallow in your own self-rejection!

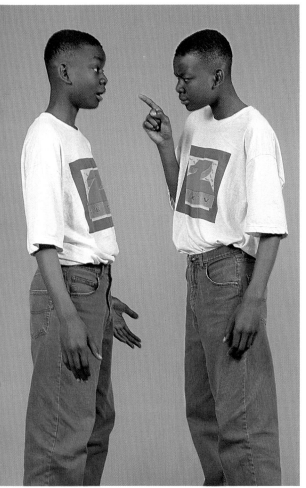

Constantly putting yourself down is self punishment which offers no solution. Remember that to God you, in your guilty state, were worth dying for.

depressed. And God seems a long way away.

Not even a question, just a statement. It's hard even to begin to answer since you don't give much information. Certainly you express a tension between your spiritual life and your girl-friend relationship. Maybe you don't share the same

13

The God of hope and healing

Therefore, if anyone is in Christ, he is a new creation; the old has gone, the new has come! 2 Corinthians 5:17, NIV.

FORGIVENESS IS NOT ENOUGH

Forgiveness is not enough! It may sound strange even to say that, since we usually think of our Christian beliefs in terms of God's forgiveness for our sins. Yet if we just leave it there, we miss the point, and we don't progress in our Christian experience. In fact we can even make a mockery of the whole plan of salvation!

As someone once said, 'I wish I could die right after confession!' The idea that the slate is wiped clean, so if we die then, we have our salvation guaranteed! Or, as we've also heard: 'Lord, take me when I've remembered to ask for forgiveness of all my sins.' Seen in those terms God becomes a divine checker of sin who is busy making sure that every last sin has been forgiven on a cosmic score-card. Salvation becomes the process of making sure every sinful action has a balancing 'forgiven' marked against it.

And this idea can even lead us to be casual about sin. One man we spoke to didn't seem to be bothered about his sins in any way. Even some serious sexual sins. 'After all,' he told us, 'God's in the forgiveness business!' This is why Paul had to write in such strong terms to the folk in Rome who were wondering whether they should 'continue in sin so that grace may abound.' God forbid! said Paul. Absolutely not! (see Romans 6:1.)

Why not? Because while God can and does forgive, that's only part of His goal.

God's plan is not just to have a people who are legally not guilty, pardoned, forgiven. When Jesus' birth was announced, He was to be called Jesus not because He would forgive His people their sins but because He would *save* His people *from* their sins! (see Matthew 1:21.)

To be forgiven is not enough for God. He wants us saved *from* our sins — from the results, the pain, the death of sin. And that's particularly relevant in sexual sin, which is so destructive of personal relationships.

That's why God is identified in Psalm 103:3 as the One who *forgives all your iniquities, heals all your diseases*. In the Hebrew parallelism of the poetry of the Psalms, the forgiving of sins is identified with healing — which is what Jesus did in His ministry too (see for example Luke 5:20-24). Not only does God want to forgive our sins, but reclaim us from them. That's why David prays to God, not just to be forgiven, but for God to create a new heart in him, and renew a right spirit within him (see Psalm 51:10).

That is why forgiveness is called God's *remedy* for sin. It is the *cure* of sin, not just some way of saying sin is legally taken care of. God is *restoring* us, making us new again. 'Therefore, if anyone is in Christ, he is a new creation; the old has gone, the new has come!' (2 Corinthians 5:17, NIV.) For everyone who looks at his life and sees a total mess and so much guilt, this is a wonderful assurance!

Restoration. Cure. Healing. Remaking God's image in us. That's

what God wants to do, not to have us come to Him and say, 'Please forgive me' and once we are forgiven go on in our own way. God is far more interested in taking away our desire to sin than in just taking away specific sins!

That's why, when Peter asked Jesus about forgiveness, he missed the point. The Jews said forgive five times. Peter, in saying seven times, thought he was being extra generous. But Jesus' 'seventy times seven' expresses the kind of *attitude* that real forgiveness is all about. And that's why we must not limit God's forgiveness.

Forgiveness provides the inspiration to leave behind the ashes of guilt and gives restoration to life and relationship.

Jesus told the parable of the ungrateful servant to explain what He meant, and concluded that we are to forgive one another 'from your heart' (in other words, not keeping count and taking record, but having the right spirit).

We too must do this. Jesus is not just saying God's forgiveness is limitless and ours should be too — but that there's something more important than being forgiven. It's being *saved* and *healed* from sin — so that ultimately we won't need to be forgiven any more, because we won't want to go on sinning!

In the story Jesus told Simon the hypocrite (see Luke 7:36-50) when the 'immoral woman' anointed Jesus' feet, the punchline is: "'Therefore, I tell you, her many sins have been forgiven — for she loved much. But he who has been forgiven little loves little.'" (Luke 7:47, NIV.)

Simon begins to see the immensity of his guilt. In the same way as a debt of 500 is ten times 50, so his guilt was that much greater. And when Simon admitted it, and heard Jesus' commendation, he began to realize how wrong his attitude was to God and His forgiveness.

Then Jesus goes on to say what the woman has done. For true forgiveness brings *results*. Her actions for Jesus expressed what she felt in her heart: her great love for Him, her amazement that Jesus should even consider one like herself, her overwhelming gratitude for the heal-

Sexual sin in others is often considered the worst by those who have no sense of their own shame and guilt.

ing, forgiving God in Christ. (Remember her reputation was as a sinner, and the implication of the story is that she was sexually immoral.) In contrast Simon's lack of attention and care show his coldness, and how little he really appreciated what Jesus had done for him. For though he had been healed from his leprosy, he had not really experienced God's healing salvation.

So it is to the woman that Jesus speaks the words, '"Your faith has saved you; go in peace."' (Luke 7:50, NIV.) Simon sees God's great compassion shown to someone he had written off as being impossible to save. And deep in his heart he realizes that he is in greater need of forgiveness because of the hardness of his heart. Accepting God's forgiveness and healing for himself, Simon becomes one of Jesus' disciples; a proud Pharisee changed into a humble, self-sacrificing follower of Jesus. The result of God's great healing forgiveness!

So what about you? Maybe you have said that forgiveness is not enough, especially when you keep on coming back asking to be forgiven for some repeated sin.

On the other hand, it's hard even to accept it — like Simon, we may even think we're reasonably 'OK'. Or we may not feel able to accept such merciful forgiveness. We may believe in God as a forgiving God, but not be able to forgive ourselves.

Perhaps you're like the woman we know who was still asking God for forgiveness thirty years on from the time she'd sinned, never able to believe she was forgiven. The truth is that as soon as we sincerely ask for forgiveness, God forgives.

FINDING THE CURE

The forgiveness that God offers also involves the cure. He is not only interested in dealing with the symptoms, He wants to heal the disease. We need to see God not just as some heavenly book-keeper who keeps track of your sins, but the Divine Physician who wishes to heal you from all your diseases (see Psalm 103:3).

As Christians, we know we are not supposed to go on sinning. And yet we still do. So what is the solution? How can we be right when we are so often wrong? Speaking of Jesus, John writes: 'He is himself the remedy for the defilement of our sins . . . .' (1 John 2:2, NEB.) As God changes us, remakes us into His image, then the guilt and stain of the disease of sin is taken away, and we are made spiritually healthy.

God's desire for all of us is to be right with one another and one with Him. In order to do that we have to come to the only one who can help us. And forgiveness in this case is not enough. When we are sick and go to the doctor, he doesn't say, 'I forgive you.' He attempts to provide a cure. In just the same way, when we are spiritually sick, God doesn't say, 'I forgive you.' Rather He enters in and begins the process of change and healing, making us well again.

Because even if we should refuse His help, and eventually die, just like a doctor who goes to the funeral of a patient who refused his help, God may still be saying, 'I forgive you' — but we will be dead. Forgiveness can never be enough, it must lead us to that oneness with God that is eternal life. For, 'If we confess our sins, he is faithful and just and will forgive us our sins and purify us from all unrighteousness.' (1 John 1:9, NIV.)

THE GOD OF HOPE

We need to go back to Eden — the original and best! The way that God intended a man and a woman to relate to each other, in a perfect world. Now the world is far from perfect today, and we all bear different scars of sin. But we are still called back to the sexual ideal that God gave to Adam and Eve:

'''At last, here is one of my own kind — Bone taken from my bone, and flesh from my flesh. 'Woman' is her name because she was taken out of man.'' That is why a man leaves his father and mother and is united with his wife, and they become one. The man and the woman were both naked, but they were not embarrassed.' (Genesis 2:23-25.)

We need to understand the specialness of God's extraordinary gift of human sexuality. That male was made for female, and the other way too, means there is so much to be explored together. Sex is not really about the physical act, though that is important. Nor is it about being a sexual athlete, or having good technique. It's about being sensitive to each other, and finding out how to please each other in a warm relationship that is much more than genital contact. It's saying to the other person, 'You are the most important person in the world for me.' Sex, as designed by God, can't be separated from that great love between one man and one woman.

The wonderful experience of sex celebrates not only God the giver of physical pleasure, but the One who made sex to be part of the expression of all parts of a complete relationship — of being one. And maybe that's where Christians have most to learn. To see that sex is not wrong or dirty or in any way less than good. The idea of allowing yourself to 'lose control' in the arms of another makes some fear that they would displease God. But this is not so, for God made the sexual act to be just that. In that situation you are most vulnerable — naked and totally trusting. And that says much about our gracious God.

And that also shows how trivial having sex with someone in a casual way really is. You are throwing God's gift in His face, and saying you don't really value it. Like a child playing with an expensive gold watch down in the stones and dirt

Agreement on the objectives of your life together is essential. Many rely on 'love' and sex to hold their relationship together, but so often it falls apart when stress and problems inevitably arrive.

— it's soon damaged and defaced. For making love in marriage is a 'sacrament' — a kind of worship. That's why in the old marriage service were the lines 'with my body I thee worship'. You 'worship' — give each other worth — through the mental, emotional, spiritual and physical aspects of human sexual love. And in this you worship the God who gave it all.

Jesus took us back to that ideal, that hope for every Christian, when He answered the sad question about divorce — reminding His hearers of what marriage *should* be like:

'"Haven't you read," he replied, "that at the beginning the Creator 'made them male and female', and said, 'For this reason a man will leave his father and mother and be united to his wife, and the two will become one flesh'? So they are no longer two, but one. Therefore what God has joined together, let man not separate.''' (Matthew 19:4-6, NIV.)

The God of Hope hopes for you, and wishes for you that 'one flesh' experience of which sex is just a part. And much of how this will be true for you depends on the way you view sexuality, and God's role in it. Don't leave God outside your intimate relationship, but make Him the centre of hope for your marriage.

GOD'S PROMISE AND YOURS

What is God's promise to you? That He will be with you wherever you go, and to watch over you — as He promised Jacob so long ago (see Genesis 28:15). But what God can do will be limited by what you yourself choose. That's why in all areas of life, especially in intimate relationships, the right choices are so important.

We don't know what choices you have already made. You may be starting out, and looking out uncertainly on all that is ahead of you. You are perhaps beginning the sexual journey. You may have already 'gone too far'. All we can say is that God has promised to be with you whatever your situation, to be the Friend that sticks closer than a brother (see Proverbs 18:24).

What does the future hold for you? As you think of life, and choosing a partner, God's promise is that He can be there to make it good — even very good. There are no guarantees, of course. He cannot 'arrange' for the girl of your dreams to come alive, and to fall hopelessly in love with you. But with God at the centre of a committed marriage, there is much more to hope for than if God is not there.

Not, as we have already said, that marriage must be seen as the only objective. To be single and keep your relationship with God is surely wiser than marriage without God. And even in Christian marriages there are hard times, and even failure.

However, we can't tell God to do what we are not prepared to do ourselves; to make marriage the best it can be. He will not force us against our wills, and in marriage both husband and wife keep their freedom of choice. That's why it always remains true that you do have to work to keep the relationship good. You cannot take it all for granted, or assume that just because you are both Christians that there will be no disagreements or troubles. How you build your relationship is up to you. And in that relationship, your sexual

> **Write out your promise to God. What you will do. What you will not do. And ask God to help you keep your promise to Him.**

journey together will be important. You need to talk about it, please each other, respect each other and most of all, make sure that all is done with the highest principle — unselfish love.

That's why marriage was designed by God. It's a safe area where husband and wife can be themselves. It's not just a piece of paper or a formal ceremony. Marriage is the recognition — by husband and wife and society — that these two people have made a life-time commitment to each other, and only to each other. What keeps a marriage together is what starts a marriage — the giving of complete trust. That's why 'affairs' — sex outside of marriage — are so damaging. They destroy trust, and kill the heart of marriage. That's not to say that the marriage is doomed. Many still stay together, despite the pain and hurt. But the relationship can never be the same again.

So we appeal to you. Keep yourself as the best gift you can ever be for your wife. A wedding is more than gowns and bridesmaids and receptions. The wedding is used by God to illustrate the relationship He wants to have with His faithful people.

That's God's ideal for you. So what about you? What do you *really* want? A quick 'fling'? A series of unsatisfactory physical encounters? Or a life-long love that is truly divine? Only with God will this be possible. We wish for you God's

richest blessing in your life, and the wisdom to choose the very best — God's only way.

INDEX

Page numbers in italics indicate diagrams

Abilities 63, 79
Abortion 9, 18, 152, 153
Abuse 13, 123, 136
Acceptance 21, 59
Adolescence 21, 139, 144
Adultery 28, 91, 108, 138, 144, 145, 174
Adulthood 21, 24, 149
Affair 156
Affection 39, 79
Africa 149
AIDS (Acquired immune deficiency
    syndrome) 9, 42, 75, 112, 148, *149*,
    149-151, 158-163
Alcohol 13, 22, 92, 122
Antibiotics 147
Anus *36*
Anxiety 24, 156
Aphrodisiacs 54
Arousal, sexual 56, 57
Arthritis 147
Assurance 65
Attraction 39
Attractiveness 28, 30, 63

Baby 16, 38, 39, 90, 112, 147, 152, 153
Bacterial infection 147
Beauty 57, 60, 63, 79, 94, 118, 141
Behaviour, girl-friend's 63
Bestiality 144
Bladder *36*
Blindness 123, 147
Blood 148, 150
    transfusion 159, 160
Body's defences 149
Body fluids 148
Bowel 158
Brain 147, 158
Breasts 15, 34, 39, 58, 94, 95, 106, 141
Broken sex 144, 175
    self-esteem 145

Brothel 88
Buttocks 15, 141

Cancer 147, 150, 158
Caressing 22, 58, 94, 106
Casual sex 148, 165
Celibacy 86-88, 144, 160
Cervical cancer 147
Character 63
Childhood 20, 148
Children 88, 112, 151, 158-162
Chimpanzees 148
Chlamydia 147
Circumcision 36
Clap, the 146
Clitoris 36, 41
Commitment 43, 54, 57, 65, 154
Common cold 158
Compassion 74
Computer porn 142
Concentration 156
Conception 86, 152, 153
Condoms (sheath) 148, 150, 154, 159, 162
Confidant/counsellor 103
Conjunctivae 147
Conscience 106
Contraception 51, 112, 152, 154, 157
Contraceptive pill 10, 154, 162
Corpus cavernosum *36*
    spongiosum *36*
Courtship 65, 115
Cowper's gland *36*
Cross-infection 157
Cuddling 43, 65, 104, 107, 116

Date rape 126
Dating 65, 66
Daydreams 21, 22
Death 42, 146, 148, 150, 162, 169
Decisions 50, 71
Dementia 158

Depression 156
Diaphragm, for contraception 154
Diarrhoea 150, 158
Diseases 42, 51, 54, 68, 76, 110, 112, 146,
    147, 150, 152, 154, 158, 162, 163, 181
Distractions 102
Divorce 54, 183
Doubt 24
Dreaming 21, 22, 37, 50, 82, 125, 132, 134
Drinking alcohol 13, 22, 92, 122
Drug addicts 148
Drugs 22, 147, 148, 160, 162, 163

Ecstasy, sexual 111
Effeminate 143
Egg (ovum) 38, *38*, 39, 41
Ejaculation 37, 38, 41, 51, 129
Embarrassment 22, 30, 35
Emotion 68, 125
Emotional consequences 154
Engagement 17, 43, 51, 69, 75, 99
Enjoyment in marriage 117
Entertainment 101
Epididymis *36*
Erection of penis 35-37
Erotic dreams 37
Eroticism 49, 123
Excitement 10, 28, 44, 49, 57, 142
Experimentation 26, 43

Facial infection 147
False negatives (AIDS) 150
    positives (AIDS) 150
Fantasizing 10, 18, 21, 22, 32, 47, 50, 122,
    123, 125, 127, 130, 132-134, 142, 145
Fashion 9
Fatherhood 153
Fear 22, 24, 41
Female reproductive system *38*
Fertilization 39
Fever 147, 152
Fiancée 151
Flushes, body 40
Foetus *38*
Fondling 39, 106
Foreplay 51
Foreskin of penis 36
Forgetfulness 156

Forgiveness 130, 166, 167, 169, 171, 172,
    174-178, 180-182
Fornication 108
Friendship 25, 28, 29, 34, 56, 82, 100, 103,
    108, 132
Frigidity 51
Fulfilment 36
Fun sex 70, 146

Gardnerella vaginalis 148
Gay gene, the 143
    person 51, 104, 139
General lassitude 156
Genetic disorders 153
Genital blisters 147
    herpes 147
    organs *36*, 36-40, 58, 103
    sex 103, 104, 115, 120, 121, 129, 165, 182
    sores 152
    stimulation 106, 120, 121
    warts 147
Genito-urinary clinics 152
Girlie magazines 105
Glands, swollen 147
Glans penis *36*
Gonorrhoea 122, 146, 163
Gratification 88, 122
Greed 113
Grief 68
Guilt 24, 28, 29, 41, 58, 74, 85, 96, 110-112,
    114-117, 122, 126, 145, 154, 157, 162-165,
    167, 169, 171, 177, 178, 180, 181

Haemophiliacs 162
Hard-core porn 100
Headache 147, 152, 156
Heart 147
Heartbreak 58
Hereditary disease 162
Herpes virus 147, 158
Heterosexuality 12, 140, 144, 159
HIV (Human immunodeficiency virus) 148,
    149, 151, 158-160
Holding hands 57
Homophobia 144
Homosexuality 18, 21, 22, 104, 138-140,
    142-144, 149, 159
Honesty 59, 152

Hormones 37, 52, 143
Hugging 115
Hygiene 160

Immaturity 26
Immorality, sexual 71, 107, 108, 113, 115, 144
Immoral women 136
Immune system 158, 159
Impotence 12, 51
Incest 153
Indecency 113
Infatuation 56, 111, 127
Infected dentists (AIDS) 159
  mothers (AIDS) 148, 150, 159, 160
Infection 147, 148, 149, 152, 158, 159
Infidelity 108
Innocence 112
Insecurity 24
Intercourse (penetration) 13, 17, 26, 39, 40,
    41, 57, 58, 69, 84, 86, 90, 104, 106, 107,
    115, 117, 122, 127, 129, 153, 158-160,
    163
Intimacy 13, 19, 43, 44, 56, 57, 62, 65, 66,
    79, 80, 98, 102, 106, 109, 125, 126, 130,
    140, 142, 158, 184
Intravenous drug users 149, 159
IUD (Intrauterine device) 154

Jilted 69
Joints 147

Kaposis sarcoma 150
Kidneys 147
Kissing 13, 34, 39, 40, 43, 58, 62, 65, 71, 80,
    94, 104, 106, 107, 109, 115, 116, 120,
    157

Legs 141
Liver 147
Love confusion 59
  at first sight 65
  relationship 66, 69
Loyalty 59
Lust 15, 28, 56, 71, 74, 75, 87, 93, 94, 104,
    118, 120, 122, 127, 128, 132, 135, 139,
    141, 145, 164
Lymph glands, cancer of 150

Magazines 9, 49, 67, 100, 105, 135, 145
Making out 57
Male reproductive system *36*
Manhood 20, 30
Marital breakdown 74
Marriage 9, 17, 20, 22, 26, 28, 33, 41-43, 49,
    51, 58-60, 62, 65, 66, 69, 74-77, 86-88,
    90, 91, 96, 97, 99, 104, 110-115, 117,
    120-123, 125, 137, 145, 150, 152,
    160-162, 165, 176, 183-185
Masturbation 17, 18, 37, 39-41, 49, 57, 85,
    104, 107, 115, 120-125, 129, 130, 133,
    142, 165
Maturity 24, 64, 125
Menstruation (periods) 10, 51, 120
Mental consequences 154
Misunderstanding 83
Monkeys 148
Morality 18
Morals 44, 76, 79
Motherhood 153
Movies 9, 12, 67
Murder 128, 145, 175

Necking 57
Needle, shared 148, 159, 160, 162
Nocturnal emissions 37
Normal relationships 19, 21, 134
Nudity 86, 121, 142

Obsessive sex 132
Open sores 147
Oral infection 147
  sex 18, 39-41, 85, 107, 115, 120-122, 129,
    165
Orgasm 10, 39-41, 103, 121, 129, 165
Orgies 92
Orphaned children 151, 158
Outward appearance 63
Ovaries *38*, 39
Ovum (egg) 39

Parasite 158
Passion 28, 48, 52, 71, 94, 116, 138
Patience 74
Penetration (intercourse) 40, 129
Penicillin 147
Penis 25, 35-37, *36*, 40, 105, 129, 146

Periods (menstruation) 10, 51, 120
Permissive society 12, 86, 90
Pervert 130
Petting 17, 39, 40, 57, 58, 116
Physical contact 57
　involvement 115
　relationship 116
　sex 68
Pill, contraceptive 10, 154, 162
Pleasure 10, 15, 22, 37, 39, 41, 68, 75, 77,
　84, 86, 88, 96, 99, 105, 112, 115, 122,
　123, 132, 172, 182
Pneumonia 150
Pop songs 9
Pornography 9, 22, 49, 99, 100, 118, 120,
　123, 132-135, 140-143
Post-coital depression 41
Pregnancy 18, 38, 41, 51, 68, 75, 76, 85, 110,
　121, 147, 149, 152, 153, 162
Premarital sex 67, 99, 111, 116, 117, 130, 160
Prepuce 36
Prevention 156
Priapism 37
Priesthood 86
Principles 76, 105
Process of discovery 64
Promiscuity 108, 130
Prostate gland 36
Prostitution 9, 71, 113, 120, 135-137, 141, 172
Puberty 37

Rape 105, 121, 123, 126-130, 143, 151, 153
Rapid breathing 40
Rectum 36
Religion 10, 15, 62
Repentance 166
Reproduction 39, 84
Respect 59
Responsibility 59
Romance 78, 81-83, 115

Sadness 58
Safe sex 148, 159, 160
Scare tactics 123
Scrotum 36, 37
Selfishness 60
Self-esteem 30, 145, 154, 157
　-worth 24, 117

Semen 37, 38, 41, 123, 148
Seminal fluid 37
　vesicles 36, 37
Sensation, sexual 36, 52
Sensitivity 24
Sensuality 10, 57
Sexaholic 13
Sex crimes 9
　manuals 165
　phone lines 142
　tourism 9
Sexual abuse 13, 123, 136, 143, 151
　addiction 133-135
　arousal 56, 57
　awareness 134
　crime 123
　drive 43, 44, 57, 134
　ecstasy 111
　ethics 165
　excitement 10, 28, 44, 49, 57, 142
　experimentation 66
　exploration 117
　expression 22, 58
　fantasies 10, 18, 21, 22, 32, 47, 50, 122,
　　123, 125, 127, 130, 132-134, 142, 145
　frustration 129
　fulfilment 36
　images 135
　immorality 93, 94, 159
　organs 35, 38, 58
　perversions 22, 136, 137
　phobias 165
　pleasure 135
　practice 129
　problems 133
　relationship 154
　satisfaction 50, 51
　secretions 148
　signals 118
　sins 98
　skills 165
　stimulation 36, 37, 39, 41, 58, 105, 106,
　　121, 122, 135
　stimuli 9
　substitutes 122
　technique 165
　tension 129
　union 57

violence 133
Sexually active 26
  -obsessive behaviour 132
  -transmitted diseases 112, 136, 146-148, 152, 162, 163
Sex with an animal 137
  with another man 137, 138
  with close relatives 137, 144
Sex, wrong 70
Shame 157
Shyness 22, 30
Simulated sexual intercourse 39, 41
Sinful desire 130
Skin cancer 158
  diseases 150
  , virus attack 158
Sleeping around 33, 59, 99, 111, 162
Sleeplessness 156
Smoking 122
Solo-sex 129
Sores, genital 152
Special clinics 152, 162
Sperm 37-39, *37*, *38*, 41
Spinal cord 147
Spiritual decline 42
  demension 68, 106
  relationship 68, 82
Sport 50, 124
Sterility 147, 148
Stimulants 22
Stomach infections 150
Suicide 169
Sweating 152
Swollen glands 147
Symphysis *36*
Syphilis 147, *147*, 148, 163

Temptation 16, 17, 32, 58, 72, 75, 76, 85-87, 101, 103, 106-109, 114, 116, 118, 125, 130, 135
Tenderness 116
Terror 24
Testicles 37
Testes *36*
Testosterone hormone 37
Thrush 148
Tiredness 150
Togetherness 58

Touching 17, 22, 39, 57, 58, 79, 106, 129, 130, 159
Transfusion of infected blood 159
Trichomonas vaginalis 148
Trivial sex 13, 14
Trust 42, 59, 65, 66, 77, 127, 145, 152, 157, 171
Truthfulness 59, 74
TV 9, 70

Unnatural practices 139
Unpardonable sin 169
Unprotected sex 42
Urethra *36*
Urethritis 148
Urination 147
Unselfishness 74
Uterus (womb) *37*, *38*, 39

Vaccine 158
Vagina 36, *38*, 40, 41, 129
Values 76
Vas deferens *36*
Venereal disease 146, 163
Vice 100
Victimless crime 156
Videos 9
Violence 126, 127, 130, 143
Virginity 17, 26, 33, 48, 49, 51 110, 116, 160
Virus 147-151, 158-160
Visual signals 135
  stimulation 118, 123, 135

Walk-in clinics 152
Warts, genital 147
Weakness 25
Weight loss 150, 158
Wet dreams 37
Whores 141
Wife 72, 116
Womb (uterus) *37*, *38*, 39, 42
Wrong sex 70

Zygote *38*

PHOTOGRAPHERS